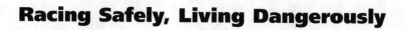

**Racing Safely, Living Dangerously**

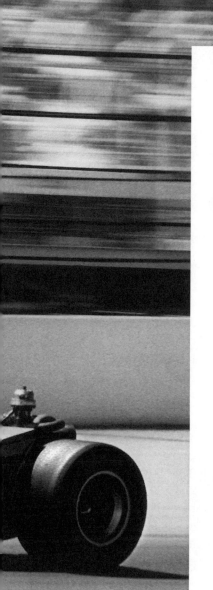

Racing Safely,
# Living
# Dangerously

## The Hard Life
## and Fast Times of a
## Motorsports Mogul

By Bill Simpson
With Bones Bourcier

PERFORMANCE MEDIA

ISBN 0-89272-518-4
Library of Congress Catalog Card Number: 00-107145

Book Design by Gay Kempton
Printed and bound at Versa Press, East Peoria, Ill.

2    4    5    3    1

Performance Media books are distributed by
Down East Enterprise
P.O. Box 679
Camden, Maine  04843

Book orders: 1-800-766-1670

# Contents

# FOREWORD: Thanks Again, Bill

By Rick Mears
Four-time Indianapolis 500 winner; three-time CART champion

I was never the kind of race driver who got up every day looking for an opportunity. What I mean is, I never did anything with the idea that it might help me get somewhere. I always figured that if you love what you do and you do a good job at it, the rest of it is going to take care of itself.

For years I've had kids come up and ask, "What do I have to do to get to Indianapolis?" To me, that's the wrong approach. If you simply put your best foot forward, with a little bit of luck your effort will be noticed. And once you start getting noticed, opportunities will come. That's just the way it works.

Looking back, Bill Simpson was my first really big opportunity.

I still remember meeting him. I was living in Bakersfield, California, and I'd had a fair amount of success in off-road racing. Simpson was already a well-known guy; he was driving Indy cars and doing a bit of road racing, and his safety company had already been around for a long time. In fact, Simpson had been backing me as a product sponsor, one of the earliest sponsors I had, but through all my dealings with his company I had never met Bill. Then, early in 1975, I went to one of the big trade shows. I was with a guy named Steve Richards, who was the Simpson rep at the off-road races.

Steve said, "Let me introduce you to Bill."

We walked up to where Simpson was standing. He was looking in the other direction, with his back to us. Just about the time we got there, Bill turned around. He saw me with Steve and he said, "Don't tell me. This is another one of those blankety-blank off-road racers."

That made a hell of a first impression on me.

9

I'm not sure what kind of impression I made on Bill, though, because a while later I was at his factory, in Torrance, California, and he happened to walk in. He looked at me for a second, said "Hi"—that's it, just "Hi"—and kept right on going. He came in through one door and went out another, and I'm still not sure if he knew who I was.

But the third time I ran into Bill was the occasion that cemented our relationship. I was getting away from the off-road stuff a bit and doing some road racing with the Sports Car Club of America, and we had gone to Willow Springs, a track in California, to test our Super Vee car. Bill was there too, trying out a new Formula 5000 car. I was making a few adjustments between test runs, and I heard this voice: "Hey, Mears!"

I looked up, and here came Bill Simpson, walking down the pit lane and greeting me like he'd known me for 10 years. He took me over to look at his car, and we chatted a while. Then we both got back to work, he running his F5000 car and me testing my Super Vee. The next morning I went back to my day job, operating a backhoe for my dad's construction company.

A short time later, maybe a week, I got a phone call. It was Simpson. He said, "What are you doing next Wednesday?"

I said, "Working."

"Can you get the day off?"

"I guess so. Why?"

"I want you to test my Formula 5000 car."

I said, "Sure, I can definitely take the day off."

When Wednesday came, we went back to Willow Springs and I made some laps. That was the first big-horsepower race car I had ever driven; in fact, other than a short-track car I ran in Bakersfield, I'd never driven anything with V-8 power. I loved the feeling of the engine and the car, and I guess I did all right. Bill drove the car too, and by the end of the day I had gone quicker than he had.

We were both happy about the way things went, and, well, everything kind of took off from there.

Bill said, "I'd like to sign you up."

I didn't know what to say. But I remember thinking, Sign me up? I've never had a contract for anything in my life!

We made a deal that included me driving for him in F5000 and/or Indy cars. It was a huge step for me, but again, I never looked at things that way. I think I viewed it more like, Hey, this is great! I get to drive something different.

I did a few F5000 races in '75 with Bill, just club-level SCCA events, and for most of the next year I wondered to myself when I might get to drive the Indy car. Then one day Bill called and said he had sold his second Indy car, a Gurney Eagle that was a few years old, to a fellow named Art Sugai. When I heard that, I didn't know where I stood. But then Bill said, "I told Art the only way I'd sell it to him is if he lets you drive it." Then he mentioned that before he turned it over to Sugai, he was going to run it one last time, in the 1976 California 500, at the old Ontario Motor Speedway. And he told me it was my ride if I wanted it.

You bet I wanted it.

So in my very first Indy car race, Bill Simpson was my boss and my teammate.

The thing I remember most about that California 500 is getting the green flag and thinking, There's Mario Andretti. There's A.J. Foyt. There are the Unsers. These are real people, not supermen. They put their pants on one leg at a time, just like I do. Once I realized that, I was able to go racing with them.

My goal at Ontario was to run hard and not make any mistakes, and it worked out pretty well. We finished eighth, and after the race Simpson and Art Sugai went their separate ways. I went with Art and the car, but I maintained my relationship with Bill because I continued to wear his safety gear. In fact I wore Simpson's stuff for my entire career, from the dune buggies through all the Indy car success with Roger Penske's team. It may have been one of the longest driver-manufacturer associations in the sport. I liked the way Bill was so hands-on; he was always at the tracks, always available, and I think that helped make him what he is today.

I can also tell you this: There were many times when I was thankful for having him on my side. One was when I had the biggest crash of my life, at Indianapolis in '92, while practicing for the 500. A radiator pipe broke and dumped a lot of coolant on my right rear tire. That spun me into the wall, and the impact flipped the car. I ended up sliding down the track with my helmet scraping along the asphalt. It was a Simpson, as always, and it did its job.

From what they tell me, I used that helmet up. But I can't say for sure; the last time I saw it was when I strapped it on for that practice run. After a big crash like that, the track crew sometimes takes your gear, and then the officials look it over and who knows where it goes from there? I guess Bill probably has the helmet today, and that's OK with me.

I retired from driving at the end of the 1992 season, but I continue to play an advisory role with Team Penske, so I still see Simpson from time to time. It's nice to sit down and have a beer with him, and kick around some memories. He has become a hell of a good friend.

Now that he's gotten away from the day-to-day operation of his company, he seems more relaxed than he used to be. It's like a load has been lifted off his shoulders, and I'm glad for him. Bill has always been known for his ability to have a good time and to, shall we say, enjoy life . . . and I think it's great that he's able to spend more time doing that. He has certainly earned it.

Simpson has stuck around for a long time, through thick and thin, because he loves this sport and the people in it. And one thing is sure: That man has left quite a mark on automobile racing. A lot of people are grateful that he came along. I can say that with some authority, because I'm one of them.

A couple of hours after my fourth win at Indianapolis, in 1991, my wife, Chris, and I stopped by Simpson's suite. I wanted to thank him, to let him know how much I appreciated him opening that door for me in 1976. And now I find myself doing that again.

Thanks, Bill.

# INTRODUCTION: One Hell of a Subject

By Bones Bourcier

When word first began to get around that Bill Simpson and I were collaborating on his autobiography, the thing I heard most, everybody's little joke, was this: "You're going to end up with a hell of a book—if you survive." Meaning, of course, that spending as much time with Simpson as it would take to chronicle his colorful life was not going to be a day at the beach. I heard this from race drivers, from mechanics, from team owners and from Simpson's closest friends, and I paid attention. These were the voices of experience.

I understood the warnings. Anybody who has run with Simpson for any length of time can tell you about his nonstop pace. Working or playing, he is a man with only two speeds: flat-out and asleep. And he doesn't sleep much. He is not an easy man to keep up with.

Well, I'm happy to say that I survived. And, if you'll forgive me this one small boast, I do think we ended up with one hell of a book.

Of course Bill Simpson is one hell of a subject.

Right up front, I ought to acknowledge this: I came late to the Simpson party. We did not formally meet until 1994, when I went to North Carolina to interview him for a magazine story. By then he was already a huge figure in motorsports (hence the magazine's interest in him) and he had long since done all the things that made him Bill Simpson: the hell-raising, the race-driving, the safety pioneering, all of it. We sat down in a restaurant north of Charlotte, did the interview, and then dove into a few rounds of drinks. We discovered that we had a handful of mutual friends, and in no time at all we were friends too. No, not friends in the way that he and Don Prudhomme are friends, or he and Rick Mears, or he and Parnelli Jones, because those men and others share with Simpson a rich history I was born too late to be a part of. But friends nonetheless. I just plain liked the guy.

There was more to it than that. I had an old-fashioned respect for the fact that, in racing, Simpson had been there and done that. Bill came out of the 1960s, an era that has always held a great fascination for me, and he is one of a handful of men who literally raced their way from poverty all the way to the most glamorous tracks in the country—and built a world-renowned business along the way.

I always tried to spend my time around Simpson with my mouth shut and my ears open, soaking in the old-days stories the way you should whenever you're in the company of a big guy. As the years and the stories rolled along, one comment kept popping up in the conversations, over and over again, in pit areas and gin mills and VIP suites: "Simpson, you really ought to do a book."

It became something he and I would discuss occasionally, the idea of me sitting down with him and helping him turn his extraordinary stories into words on a printed page, but neither of us had the time that required. So the project had to wait.

Eventually, by early 1999, Simpson had sold a chunk of his company, which relaxed his work schedule a bit, and the two magazines for which I'd done most of my writing changed hands, which freed me from the monthly deadlines that always made larger projects impractical.

"Why don't we get started on that book?" Bill asked me one day.

"Let's do it," I said.

Defining our roles took no time at all. Bill would talk; I would listen and record and take notes. Bill would drop the names of people he thought could provide information and anecdotes; I would track them down.

Thus began hours and hours of interviews, the first of which took place in the back of his Learjet on a midnight flight to North Carolina. We had just rung the curtain down on a rowdy St. Patrick's Day party at Kelly's Pub Too, Bill's favorite Indianapolis saloon. Interrogating Bill Simpson, it turned out, was not exactly combat duty. Across 25 years of covering automobile racing, I have conducted interviews in darkened pit areas, dusty infields, cluttered shops and cold truck cabs. It was different with Simpson. We talked aboard his airplane during full-throttle trips to Texas and Florida. We talked in his plush office, in Mooresville, North Carolina, and at his beautiful home on a quiet finger of nearby Lake Norman. We talked in his hospitality room at the Indianapolis Motor Speedway and in his condominium overlooking turn one at Lowe's Motor Speedway in Charlotte. We even talked miles off the Mexican coast, lounging on the bridge of his yacht as hundreds of dolphins playfully chaperoned us through the blue Pacific.

But if the living was easy, the work was not. Oh, Simpson was forthcoming enough. In fact his candor befits a man who has risen from absolutely nothing and absolutely nowhere to become a leader— maybe *the* leader—in his field. There are no rungs left to climb on the ladder he has chosen, so Bill Simpson doesn't need to worry about saying the right things or kissing the right behinds (actually, he never worried about any of that stuff anyway, even when it might have smoothed his path). As a result, in this book nothing comes sugar-coated. Simpson is honest, sometimes painfully so, about everything from his driving career to his crusade for racing safety to his relationships with women. On top of that, he is a splendid story-teller, one whose words require little reshaping. In those respects he was a collaborator's dream.

But this is a man who has lived such a large life that compressing it between the covers of a book took time, more time than either of us figured. There was the matter of corralling Simpson for multiple interviews—no easy task, given his restlessness. Then there was the difficult job of locating and interviewing the 30-plus friends, com-petitors and associates whose memories occasionally interrupt our text, some of whom had been out of sight, or at least out of racing, for years. But, little by little, their words came together to blend with Simpson's own, and the story took shape.

It is a story that is sometimes comic and sometimes tragic, owing to Bill's life and his times and the nature of his work. You do not live through the rugged motorsports age that produced Bill Simpson without seeing racing's good side and its bad side in equal measures.

In his prologue Simpson insists that this book is more than just his story, that it is also a chronicle of an amazing period in American racing history. I believe he's right, and I think his life serves as the perfect guide to what that period was truly like. If you think you understand hardened old warriors like Prudhomme and Parnelli and A.J. Foyt, you will understand them better after reading Simpson's account of the times in which they flourished. If you think you have a feel for the 1960s and '70s and their let-the-good-times-roll lifestyle, your feel will be more genuine once you digest Simpson's eyewitness reports. And if you think you can appreciate the dangers involved in strapping oneself into a race car, you will appreciate them more intimately after you have seen those dangers through the eyes of a man who faced them, and then did his damnedest to make them go away.

There are a hundred ways to define a hero. If you gauge racing heroism purely by the number of trophies on a man's shelf, then Simpson might not qualify; in this book he admits that, as a driver, he "wasn't a Foyt, or an Andretti, or an Unser, or a Rutherford." But the dictionary on my desk defines a hero in part as "a man celebrated for special achievements"—and on that score Simpson is a shoo-in.

Not, mind you, for those achievements that spring most quickly to mind—the technical awards he has earned, the various halls of fame in which he has been enshrined—but for an achievement far less tangible and yet far more important: Without Bill Simpson and the work he has done, a lot of racing's most public heroes might not have lived to be heroes at all.

This is a book written by, and about, a special man. It has been my privilege to be involved in it.

# Racing Safely, Living Dangerously

# PROLOGUE

Writing a book, I've found out, is pretty hard work. The decision to write this one, on the other hand, was easy. See, for years I've had people tell me I've led an amazing life, and if you hear that enough you start to look back a little bit. That brought me to this conclusion: I don't know how amazing it has been, but I sure have led a full life. There haven't been many dull moments.

I've driven in the Indianapolis 500. I've run down drag strips all over this country. I've been to every race in the world worth talking about, from the Daytona 500 to the British Grand Prix. I've known great race drivers and lousy race drivers. I've been written up in *USA Today*. I've raised some hell, and I'm still raising my share. I've dined at the Hôtel de Paris in Monte Carlo, and I've eaten breakfast in jail; one day I even had the Beatles over for lunch.

And while all this was going on, I managed to realize what became my life's goal: to be able to look back and say that I helped make automobile racing safer.

It was back in 1958 that I sewed together my first piece of safety equipment, a parachute to help slow my dragster. That chute worked, and it put me and my young company on the map. Then I branched out: driving uniforms (including the first Nomex fire suit, in 1967), gloves, shoes, helmets. What started out as Simpson Drag Chutes, a homespun business operating out of a two-bay garage in Redondo Beach, California, is now Simpson Race Products, a recognized leader in the motorsports industry with three manufacturing plants and five retail stores. We do about $40 million in sales every year,

19

and we anticipate that jumping to about $100 million pretty soon. So things have changed a little bit.

These days, every time someone writes about me in a magazine or a newspaper, they call me a "pioneer" in motorsports safety. If they think that description fits, it's all right with me. I think I've given a lot to this sport, and I know I've still got a lot left to give.

But I don't really see this book as being only about me. I see it more as a record of our time. It's partly about the stuff you see and the characters you meet if you spend enough of your life around race cars and race tracks. And it's also about all the changes that have come along in this sport, good and bad, since 1955, when I saw my first drag race, in Santa Ana, California.

We need to chronicle those changes for posterity. It's important that each new generation in this sport understands where we came from, and what the ride was like. Yeah, there's a part of me that thinks it would be pretty cool for my grandchildren to read about my life someday, but it's just as important that all these other kids learn this too. It's their history as much as it is mine. They ought to know about the people and places and times that were the foundation of this whole thing.

I'm usually too busy to reflect a lot on the past, but when I do I'm blown away. When I fell in love with racing, it wasn't exactly a highly regarded occupation. There were a bunch of us who hauled down highways like old Route 66, living from one race to the next, and it's an understatement to say that we weren't seen as first-class citizens. If we stopped at a greasy little drive-in for burgers and malts and they saw our race cars sitting outside, we had to hand over the money before the kid at the counter would even put the order in. People looked down on us; we were just bums. Today, though, if you're at the fanciest restaurant in the country and they find out you're involved in racing, it's a big thing. They want to know more, and you get treated like a VIP.

That's a hell of a change, and a bunch of us lived through it. I have a lot of friends in the racing business, and we—I say "we" because we've done this collectively—have all taken one very interesting ride. We went from being hot-rodders to hell-raisers to pretty much respectable people, and we saw a lot of cool things along the way. And I've always hoped that someone would sit down and write about those things.

I guess I ended up being the guy.

Anyway, that's why I say this book is more about the sport than it is about me. Because, see, any of the guys who came from the bottom up can tell stories just like the ones I'm going to tell you. And I sure came from the bottom, man, because there was a time when $20 was all the money in the world to me.

These days things are a little different for me. In 1998 I sold a two-thirds interest in my company to an investment banking firm, although I still serve as its chairman. It would be accurate to say that I'm comfortable. I have what I consider to be a beautiful home in North Carolina, and a house in Indianapolis. I've got a boat I escape to when I need to be someplace warm, which is fairly often. I've got a Learjet I use the way most people use their cars. There are days when I shake my head at how well things have gone for me. But I've seen the other side of that coin too, and not just in the early days.

I've been knocked upside-down and left completely broke, thanks to the lawsuit-crazy nature of this country in general and this industry in particular. Racing was, is and always will be a risky occupation, and from time to time people get hurt, or worse. That's a fact most racers accept. Still, whenever anything goes badly wrong, there's always someone—an attorney, usually—who thinks he can fix everything with a lawsuit. So everybody gets sued, from the track owner to the insurance company to the guy who manufactured the safety equipment, meaning me. It's crazy; I've spent a lifetime trying to make this game safer, yet I'm one of the first people to hear from a lawyer when something goes wrong. The legal fees I've paid would astound you, even though we've almost always been able to prove our point in court. I say almost always because some of my darkest days resulted from a legal judgment that I still think went the wrong way. That suit, in the early 1980s, brought me to my knees; but I got back up. It wasn't easy. I threw some clothes and a Hibachi grill in the trunk of my car and literally drove across the United States, meeting with my dealers and assuring them that the business would be fine and that they should stay with me. I'd stop at road-side stands and buy some vegetables, then cook 'em at night on the Hibachi. That was how I survived. And, step by step, I put things back together.

So I know about being on the bottom. I know about being in the ditch, like all racers do.

When you really look hard at it, every life is a lot like racing: You go through plenty of ups and downs. Mine has been no different. Generally speaking, things are going well for me right now. I have the freedom to do what I love most: designing new safety products and refining existing ones. For a long time, I was so busy with the day-to-day operation of the company that I didn't have time to do much R&D work. Now I do, and I feel like my creative juices are starting to flow again. That makes me awfully happy.

Still, there are days when I kick myself in the ass over the way other areas of my life have gone. I'm pretty successful as a busi-nessman, but I sure haven't been a great success in the personal side of things. I've been married three times and divorced three times, and I never spent enough time with my two sons, both of whom are now grown, when they needed a dad. I put racing and business first, and that wasn't always the right thing to do.

But I've put these personal failures in perspective, thanks to a con-versation I had not long ago with my friend Chris "The Golden Greek" Karamesines, one of the great drag racers of my era. Greek and I counted up 74 of our peers, guys we knew, who were killed in racing accidents in the 1950s and '60s. Anybody who has been around that long in any form of racing can tell you a similar story. If you came along when we did, you saw a lot of serious shit. Well, to-day we hardly ever lose a driver—it's a shock when one is killed at any major level of racing—and I know in my heart that I've helped improve that situation. And then I'll think, OK, if I had to sacrifice a bit of personal happiness for that, then maybe it was a worthwhile trade after all.

So if my life has been amazing—and I guess you'll have to be the judge of that—it's because it has been spent in an amazing sport, and in the company of some amazing people.

This book is their story, our story. And, if you love racing, your story too.

# Green Light

I was born in 1940, but there are times when I feel like my life began in 1955. That was the year Dennis Aphes, a guy who lived near me, in Redondo Beach, California, said to me, "Hey, they've got a little thing going on this weekend in Santa Ana. It's called drag racing."

I said, "Cool. What's drag racing?"

Dennis said, "Well, two cars line up side by side, and a guy drops a flag. Then the two cars haul ass for a straight quarter-mile."

I said, "I believe I'd like to see that."

So we went to Santa Ana and I was hooked right away. I mean, I thought drag racing was the greatest thing in the world.

Up until then, my life had been anything but great. My youth is something I don't talk about much, not even with my friends, because it doesn't hold a lot of pleasant memories. I grew up right there in Redondo Beach, which is a nice enough town, but it was a tough childhood. I had a brother who died young, which created a lot of stress for my parents, so they went their separate ways and eventually divorced. From the time I was about six years old, I lived apart from my mother and father. I got shuffled back and forth between my Aunt Edith's house, my Aunt Billie's house and my grandmother's house. It wasn't much of a life for a boy of that age, because I never really had a place I could call home. But that's how it was.

By the time I was 12, I was restless. Tired of bouncing from place to place, tired of the turmoil, tired of everything. I was still a kid—hell, I wasn't even a teenager yet—but every day I was dealing with grown-up problems. The way I looked at it, that made me a grown-up too. So, for better or worse, I started making my own grown-up choices about a few things. School, for one. I walked out of junior high one day when I was in the eighth grade and I never went back. I got a job setting pins at a bowling alley in Westwood, which then sounded a whole lot more appealing than reading, writing and 'rithmetic.

It wasn't the smartest decision I ever made, and there have been a hundred times in my life when a better education would have come in awfully handy. Still, the life I led as a kid provided lessons I never could have learned in a classroom, even if I'd stuck around long enough to graduate high school and then had gone to college. My youth was one long, advanced course in self-preservation, and what it taught me was this: You'd better look out for yourself, because nobody else is going to look out for you. In that regard, I'd like to believe I was an A-plus student.

Well, most of the time, anyway. I got myself in trouble at age 12 and 13, just normal adolescent-boy bullshit, and for a while I was in a kind of forestry camp for troubled kids, run by Los Angeles County. There I learned all kinds of important intellectual and social skills: how to shovel gravel, how to build roads, stuff like that.

When I was done with my tour of duty at the camp, I went back to an aunt's house, where I stayed until I was 14 or 15. Then that restless feeling returned. I moved into an apartment with a couple of older roommates, who weren't so much friends as just guys I knew, and I got a job at an upholstery factory, building sofas and chairs. I made something like $60 a week, which was pretty good money in those days, especially for a teenager.

By the time I hit 16, life had taken a definite turn for the better. It seemed like I always had a little money in my pocket, because our rent was cheap enough that my end only came to 25 or 30 bucks. Best of all, in those days you could buy a decent street car for $200. I had already been to Santa Ana, had already fallen in love with drag racing, and what my newfound wealth meant to me was this: For next to nothing, I ended up with a car that could haul me to work on weekdays, and haul me down the drag strip on the weekends.

Looking back, I see that I was the kind of kid who would have gotten into bigger and bigger trouble if something like drag racing hadn't come along to capture my attention. Actually, the sport did more than capture my attention; in no time it became my life.

Back then, California was the home office for the car culture, with a lot of gearhead types all blended together. There were the guys who raced at the drag strips, and the guys everybody called dry-lakes racers, who ran at El Mirage or Bonneville in search of top speed. Then there were the hot-rodders, who were very much into street racing. The lines between these groups were pretty blurry; a lot of the street racers also dabbled in the drags, and a lot of us drag guys also did some racing on the streets.

Hell, let's face it: *Everybody* raced on the streets.

> **Tom "Mongoose" McEwen, legendary National Hot Rod Association Funny Car racer:** *I came out of the Long Beach area, and we raced on the streets as much as we raced on the drag strips. My mom had a '52 or '53 Oldsmobile, and I used to take that out and run it at the drags when she wasn't home. And of course I raced it on the street, too. I did all that before I even had a driver's license.*

That street-racing era was made mythical by the hot-rod films Hollywood was putting out. A lot of them still play on television, particularly on that "Lost Drive-In" movie series on the Speedvision channel. In fact the theater they show in the introduction to that show was not far from where I grew up. Watching those old movies takes me back; some of them exaggerated things, but for the most part they captured the spirit of that era, which was pretty carefree.

It was a very cool time and place to be a young American male.

> **Don "Snake" Prudhomme, four-time NHRA Funny Car champion:** *It really was an incredible period. [Veteran drag racing chief mechanic] Dale Armstrong said to me one day, 'You don't realize how lucky you were to grow up out in*

*California back then, and to be surrounded by all those hot*
*rods and all that chrome and paint.' And I said, 'Geez, I never*
*thought about that. I guess I really was lucky.' Because Cali-*
*fornia, really, was the cornerstone of all that.*

Back then the West Coast was known for three things: surfing,
fast cars and pretty girls. I liked all three, especially girls and cars. To
any red-blooded male, girls and cars just went together. You know
how people talk about the "sexual revolution" that supposedly took
place in the late '60s? Well, in California we were way ahead of that.
We didn't call it a revolution, but we damn sure led it.

Like every kid I knew, I quickly got my hands on a pretty hot car,
a '40 Ford coupe. It had a bitchin' interior: white and black tuck-and-
roll upholstery, done in Tijuana. One night I was parked in that car,
passing around a quart of Pabst Blue Ribbon beer with a couple of
my buddies. I don't know why, but we had a spray can of gray
primer paint in the car. Spray paint was still a new thing, and I said,
"I wonder exactly how that stuff works." One of my pals said, "Let's
find out." He shook the can and you could hear the little steel ball
rattling inside. Then he took out one of those old church-key can
openers and stuck it into the side of the spray can. Naturally, the
thing blew up. When the cloud of paint cleared, all I could see was
the whites of this kid's eyes. The rest of him matched the new color
of my tuck-and-roll interior: gray. He looked so funny that instead of
being mad I just laughed my ass off.

On a typical Saturday night in the '50s, every badass with a fast
car would head for a hamburger stand. In my case it was the Witch
Stand, in Inglewood, but you also had The Clock, up in Culver City,
and a root beer joint down in Redondo Beach. We'd check out the
competition and then we'd all head out to some remote street. All
that mattered was that it was long enough and straight enough.

**Tom McEwen:** *We had one spot in Long Beach, on Cherry*
*Avenue near the mortuary, where we actually had a quarter-*

*mile marked off on the street with paint. We'd all meet up at Grissinger's, a hamburger place, and then head over to Cherry Avenue. It got to where we had a flagman and every-thing.*

**Don Prudhomme:** *We'd hear through the grapevine that everyone was going to meet up at 11 o'clock at night, or two o'clock in the morning, on some deserted street. Then, you know, we'd have us a drag race. There was a stretch in Bur-bank called the River Road, and we used to get it on there quite a bit. There were some great drag races there.*

All this activity helped usher in the age of aftermarket speed parts, and before long we began to see all kinds of goodies at the street races. A company called Potvin sold a kit that let you hang a supercharger on your DeSoto or Chevrolet engine. Pretty soon all the street racers had supercharged engines and cars that were more rad-ical than a lot of the ones you'd see at the drag strip.

**Tom McEwen:** *We modified our cars quite a bit. At first it was just small things, like we put a cut-out [valve] in the ex-haust; I could get underneath the car and unscrew this cap in front of the muffler. That not only made the car louder, it also gave it more power. Then we started taking the air cleaners off, and other little tricks. I put a Potvin cam in one of my Oldsmobiles, which helped it a lot. Later on I had the first '55 Chevy V-8 in Long Beach, and I put a McCullough supercharger on it. That was a fast car. I used to like to race against Corvettes. I couldn't afford a 'Vette myself, so I used to kinda go out and feast on 'em.*

One modification led to another and by 1956 or '57 some of these hot rods had full-bore race engines. Their owners would actu-ally haul their cars into town with trailers, unload them a block from the Witch Stand and fire 'em up. You could hear the roar a mile away. Then these guys would cruise into the parking lot, their engines rumbling at low idle, looking for somebody to run against.

And if the cars were wild, the mix of people was even wilder. There were kids who looked like the boy next door, rich kids from Beverly Hills, hard-edged greasers. And yet everybody got along. As long as you were into cars and hot-rodding, we figured you were cool, even if we didn't have much else in common.

> **Don Prudhomme:** *You could spot the rich kids right away because they were the ones driving the newest cars. But it was never a deal where you'd be down on a guy because maybe he had a brand-new '57 Chevy. You were just happy he came around so you could hang out with the guy and be around his car.*

It was like we were all in this thing together. There were times when we felt like we were on the fringes of society, and then there were times when it was pretty clear that society didn't accept us at all. So we kind of formed our own society, a society of street racers.

The police took a dim view of our lifestyle, which, in their defense, was pretty understandable. I mean, we were running over 100 miles per hour on the streets in the middle of the night. Round-ups were pretty routine at some of the better-known sites, like Culver Boulevard or Imperial Highway. I saw guys get hauled off by the dozens. I got pinched a couple times myself and spent a few nights in the county lock-up. Waking up in jail was just part of the deal back then.

> **Don Prudhomme:** *I got a lot of excitement out of that— you know, the thrill of the chase. I don't mean an actual police chase, with us running away from them; I mean the whole strategy of trying to elude them. We'd run a lot of our races at two or three o'clock in the morning, when we thought most of the cops were sleeping.*

*Tom McEwen: I'm lucky I never got caught, because I was around some wild shit. The wildest night I can remember from the street-racing days was over by the Long Beach Freeway, near the old Cragar plant. One of the local drag racers actually hauled his Top Fuel car out there and fired it up to race right there on the street. It was crazy. Then, of course, the cops came and everybody hauled ass like always, cutting across fields and things like that.*

What killed street racing was a two-fold deal. Number one, as the '50s rolled into the '60s, organized drag racing grew. In Southern California alone, we saw drag strips open in Saugus, San Fernando, Santa Ana, San Gabriel, Santa Maria, Half Moon Bay, Bakersfield, Hayward, Ramona and more. It just didn't make sense anymore to keep running from the cops every weekend, and risk your life on the streets in the middle of the night, when suddenly you had all these places where you could race without being hassled.

Number two, there was no getting around the fact that street racing, which was never very safe or sane to begin with, had gotten incredibly dangerous as its popularity increased. All over Southern California, there were some really terrible crashes.

*Tom McEwen: The biggest thing you worried about in street racing was somebody coming out of an intersection right in front of you. I mean, we used to do our best to block 'em all off, but accidents happened anyway.*

Eventually, the public just wouldn't tolerate this sort of thing any longer. The cops, reacting to the outcry, cracked down on street racing harder than ever. They'd hang out at the drive-ins and follow every cluster of hot rods that headed out into the night. It became just about impossible to get anything going.

So street racing died and drag racing took off. Most of the wilder characters went right along with that change. In those days drag racing had some characters you couldn't find anyplace else.

There was one guy in our crowd who figured that his car was the biggest thing in his life, so he worked on it right in his living room. That's the truth. He had a house on Western Avenue in Los Angeles, and naturally the house was bigger than the garage, so when he decided he needed more room to work on his hot rod, he simply knocked out a couple of walls, moved his tools into the house and started sleeping in the garage. The car sat in the living room, the kitchen became the engine shop, and I guess his old bedroom was where he kept his spare parts. Eventually he and his buddies ended up burning down the house. I'm not sure exactly how it happened, but the story got around that they were cleaning some parts with gasoline and the pilot light on the water heater set off the fumes.

And that guy was by no means the Lone Ranger when it came to crazy. I knew a black dude named Big Willie who used to ride his motorcycle through the front door of his apartment house and right up the stairs to the second floor, where he lived. He'd ride straight into the bedroom, climb off, lie down and go to sleep.

But this one group from Brooklyn might have taken the top prize for lunacy. They used to steal Chrysler 300s, the ones with the hot 392-cubic-inch engines, and haul 'em off to some dark corner of New York City where they'd cut the engine mounts out of the frames with torches. They used torches, you see, because it was quicker than getting the engines out with wrenches. Once they had 25 or 30 of these engines stacked up on a trailer, they'd haul the load out to California, where they'd sell the engines for a thousand bucks apiece. Then they'd head home and start the whole operation all over again.

The drag racers out on the West Coast gave those guys plenty of business. Almost every California drag car in that period was powered by a Chrysler 392, and I'll bet you most of those engines could have been traced right back to New York. None of the buyers knew for sure where that stuff came from, and they didn't *want* to know. For one thing, those Brooklyn guys were so tough you didn't want to ask 'em too many questions.

But, hell, they sort of fit right in. They were just another bunch of wide-open people in what was a wide-open form of motorsports. When you went to a drag race in the '50s, you never knew what you might see roaring down the strip. There were the earliest slingshot dragsters; there were a few different classes of heavily modified cars generically known as "altereds"; there were a half-dozen varieties of what the drag guys called "door-slammers," which was the term they hung on any production-based car; there were even some oval-track cars, roadsters that ran on the dirt at Ascot Park one night and then showed up at the drags the next night.

Because things didn't cost much money and so much of the stuff was homemade, it wasn't too hard to make your way up the drag-racing ladder. I got started in door-slammers, jumped quickly into altereds, and moved up the line into Top Fuelers while I was still a teenager. And for that whole ride, I was as crazy as the next guy.

Everyone used to fire up their cars on the side streets. It was a way to check spark plugs and check for leaks, make sure everything was ready before you loaded up to go to the drag strip. Naturally, if you happened to live in a residential area, you'd have one or two neighbors who didn't appreciate this. One Saturday morning, as I was running my dragster up and down 236th Street in Torrance, a guy came down his driveway and threw a trash can at me as I went by. It hit the front of the car and bounced right over the cockpit, which was pretty fortunate for me because I wasn't wearing a helmet.

It's not like I *wanted* to do my test runs on the same block where I lived. The simple truth is that I didn't have much of a choice. In those days you didn't leave home in the morning and go to work at the race shop, because there was no such thing as a "race shop." That term was foreign to most of us drag racers. Oh, there were some good Indy car teams around Los Angeles, and those guys operated out of garages of about four thousand square feet. That would make a decent spare-parts room at a big-time race shop today, but back then it was an unbelievable amount of space. Those of us who were less fortunate worked on our cars in our driveways or in one-bay garages.

But we didn't mind. Drag racing was our entire lives. I mean, in the 1950s, my idea of a date was having a girl sit in my garage and wash parts for me. If she did a good job, there was a second date. If the parts weren't clean enough, she was gone. That was the deal. Drag racing was more important than a relationship. Drag racing was more important than anything.

How could I not love it? It was fast and furious, it was colorful, it made a hell of a lot of noise and it just felt very aggressive. Drag racing and I had a lot in common.

# 2

# A Dangerous Game

Drag racing had something else going for it, something besides color, noise and aggression. Drag racing had danger, and I'd be lying if I said that wasn't part of its initial attraction, for me and for lots of other folks, too. I mean, nobody *wanted* to go out there and get hurt, but the fact that there were risks made racing an adventure.

I know this might sound strange coming from me, because somehow it ended up that I'd spend my life trying to eliminate those risks, but I've always felt that the presence of danger is part of what draws the type of person who becomes a racer. Even today, with racing as safe as it's become, part of the thrill is going headlong into it even though you're cognizant of the fact that you might bust your ass. It's like skydiving: If there was no danger in jumping out of an airplane, everybody would do it and it wouldn't be such a big deal.

When you built yourself a car, back then, and hauled it to the drag strip, the last thing you thought about was safety. Actually, that's not accurate. We *never* thought about safety. In the 1950s it just didn't enter your mind. It should have, because it seemed like every other week we heard about another guy getting killed on a strip someplace, but I guess that wasn't enough to wake us up.

> ***Chris Karamesines, drag-racing legend:*** *Back then we didn't have any rules about how to build a car. We just went by what we thought looked nice, or by pictures we saw in magazines. You'd start out with a [Ford] Model A chassis and just go from there. Later on, of course, we went to tube*

35

*frames, and those were stronger and safer than the Model A*
*chassis, but that's not why we started using tubing. We used*
*tubing because it was lighter, and lighter meant faster.*

We took incredible chances every time we ran down a drag strip.
If you look back at the level of safety then—and I've done that quite
a bit, especially while strolling through the National Hot Rod Association Museum, in Pomona, California—you'd think we'd have had to
be crazy. Everything right down to the very construction of the cars
was awful by today's standards. I thought my own cars were state-
of-the-art, but the fact of the matter is they were death traps. Hell, all
the cars were.

And things were even worse when it came to a driver's personal
safety gear, which was essentially nonexistent.

> **Don Prudhomme:** *We'd go to the army surplus store and*
> *buy these teardrop-shaped goggles, and Tony Nancy—a*
> *pretty famous upholstery guy out in the Valley who built*
> *some really nice roadsters—would sew a little leather mask*
> *onto the bottom of those goggles to protect your face in a*
> *flash fire. Other than that, we didn't think much about safety.*
> *When I started driving a Top Fuel car, I'd wear a leather*
> *jacket and a pair of jeans. Oh, and I'd always tuck the bot-*
> *tom of the jeans into my socks, just in case the engine blew*
> *some hot oil back onto my legs.*

Everything was substandard. The helmets sucked, the restraints
sucked. Fire suits did not exist. There was a rule about wearing seat
belts, but I don't remember anyone ever leaning into the car to
check on that. If you ran a convertible, they made you wear eye protection and some form of headgear. If you had a hardtop, they figured you had all the protection you needed.

A fellow named C.J. Hart helped run the drag races at Santa Ana, and for 25 cents he would rent you a football helmet and a pair of aviator goggles. My car was a ragtop, so I spent a lot of quarters with ol' C.J.

> **C.J. Hart, long-time drag-racing official:** *The thing was, there were no rules, and no real organization to enforce the things we should have been doing. We were literally starting from scratch, and any time you do that, you have to go through a learning process. Look at football: It's a lot safer to play football now than it was years ago. What we were doing was still brand-new.*

It was a dangerous game, but there wasn't any one particular area of concern that seemed obvious to address. The cars were evolving so fast that there was always something new that could get you hurt. Parts broke, tires blew, wheels came apart, frames collapsed. For a while we had problems with clutches blowing up so violently that they'd cut cars right in half. And sometimes they'd cut off a guy's feet, too.

Just when we'd figure out a way to address one problem, another would come up. It had a lot to do with the escalating speeds, of course; every time we'd go five miles an hour faster, we had to deal with another bugaboo. And each time we went through this, somebody ended up killed.

In retrospect, it was an awful, awful period—but at the time the danger was just something you accepted.

Understand, this wasn't just a drag-racing problem. It was the same in every other form of motorsports. All over the country you had sprint car racers and midget racers literally killing themselves trying to get to the big-time, which for them meant Indianapolis. The ones who did make it to the top didn't exactly have it easy either, because there were plenty of injuries and deaths in Indy cars too.

In the 1950s and '60s, *everything* was dangerous: stock cars, sports cars, open-wheel cars, drag cars. They all killed their share of us. So if you wanted to race you developed a cavalier attitude about life, because that was the only way to deal with it.

Let's face it, there is a lot of macho in the psychology of any race driver, then or now. Every racer has a giant ego or he wouldn't strap himself into a car to begin with. But back then, because the risk factor was so high, you had to be double-throwdown brave. Look at the men we now see as the icons of that era: Parnelli Jones and A.J. Foyt in open-wheelers, Curtis Turner and Junior Johnson in stock cars, McEwen and Prudhomme in the dragsters. To a man, those guys were hard people, the toughest of the tough.

> **Parnelli Jones, 1963 Indianapolis 500 winner:** *I don't know if we were tougher than the guys today, but we were certainly a lot dumber! No, honestly, we did look at things a bit differently. I mean, racing was a lot more dangerous then, and we lost a lot of drivers. We lived in a strange atmosphere: You saw your friends get hurt, really get hurt bad, and you knew inside that you could get hurt bad too. But you relied on the idea that your own ability would keep you from getting into trouble.*

It wasn't just machismo that made us overlook safety in those days. The truth is, we just didn't know any better. We all thought we were pretty smart guys, and some of us probably were, but safety equipment is a lot like all forms of racing equipment: Basically, it evolves by somebody looking at an existing item and figuring out a way to improve it. Back then, whatever safety equipment existed was so crude that it didn't even inspire you to say, "Hey, if we did this just a little bit better. . . ."

> **Tom McEwen:** *We didn't know what was good and what was bad. When I started drag racing, everybody wore leather.*

*They simply figured that leather was a good, tough material.*
*Well, I saw guys get burned in some bad fires and the leather*
*ended up stuck right to their skin. It was terrible. But they*
*kept on wearing it.*

Against those odds—against that ignorance—you pretty much knew you were going to bust your ass if you played around with race cars long enough. It's true what they say: What you don't know can hurt you.

My turn to be hurt by what I didn't know came one night in 1958, at San Fernando. I blew the engine in my dragster so violently that it snapped the crank. That meant I couldn't rely on engine compression to slow the car down, so I was free-wheeling. It didn't help matters much when I grabbed for the brake handle and it broke off in my hand.

At the end of the San Fernando strip, way down in the runoff area, there was kind of a makeshift dump. If you were still at speed when you got there, you were in trouble because there was junk piled everywhere. Well, I was trucking, unable to turn or stop the car, and into that mess I went. A piece of timber came right through the car; it broke both my arms and bruised the hell out of the rest of me.

As bad as it was, that crash ended up being largely responsible for whatever success I've had in my life. See, I was like most other drivers: The only time I thought about safety was after I'd been hurt. That time I was hurt badly enough to do a lot of thinking, and the most obvious thing to think about was a better way to slow down my damned car.

I started playing around with different ideas, particularly parachutes. I had never run a parachute on my dragster, but a few other guys were using war-surplus chutes, and I knew the military used parachutes to stop jet planes on short runways. I had an uncle who owned a war-surplus store; he hooked me up with a fellow who knew about parachutes. We sat and talked and I told him about the problems we were having. He listened and then he said, "You don't want to use those round parachutes, like they use for airplanes. You need a cross-form."

Of course I had no idea what the hell a cross-form was. This fellow explained that it was an experimental design, and he drew one out. It was exactly what it sounded like: a cross, like the letter X.

I said, "Man, that looks pretty simple."

And this guy said, "It is. Hell, you could probably sew these things up yourself."

That sounded crazy, because I had never in my life sewn anything together. Besides, I was a racer, not a parachute maker. But the more I looked around, the more I saw that the kind of thing I wanted wasn't readily available, and I wasn't sure if it ever would be. There were some nice guys dabbling in safety equipment in the late '50s, but they weren't very aggressive when it came to trying new things. I spoke to a few of them about parachutes, got nowhere, and finally just threw up my hands and said, "Screw this. I'll do it myself."

I found a copy of a parachute rigger's manual and studied it hard. Then I rented a sewing machine from the Alberoni Sewing Machine Company in Los Angeles. It cost me 12 bucks for three months, with a four-dollar deposit. Next I went to another place in L.A. that sold all kinds of fabrics and explained what I wanted to do. The people there recommended a material called rip-stop nylon. I hauled the fabric and the sewing machine back to my house, set everything up in my little two-car garage, and started putting parachutes together.

The first chute I made was about 30 feet in diameter, and I was real proud of it. There's a funny story that goes along with that chute. Mike Sarokin was a hot guy in drag racing at that time. He ran a dragster called the Surfer's Car for Tom Jobe and Bob Skinner, and together those guys won 72 *consecutive* Top Fuel races. Mike was also my best friend. I told him I had finished this parachute and I wanted him to help me test it. So one night Mike and I mounted the chute to the trailer hitch of my tow car, a '55 Chevy station wagon, and we headed for 190th Street in Redondo Beach.

Now, 190th Street had a huge hill; it was steep and almost a half-mile long. Our plan was to go like hell down that hill, toss out the chute, and see how much it slowed the car. Mike was driving and I was sitting in the back of the station wagon. We stopped at the top of the hill and I said, "Just floorboard this sonofabitch and holler back to me when we get close to the bottom." He gassed it and off we went.

We were hauling ass down this hill, going maybe 100 miles an hour, when I heard Mike yell: "Throw it!"

I pitched this giant-ass parachute out the back window.

The good news was that the very first parachute I ever built worked really well. The bad news was that the very first parachute I ever built worked *too* well. As soon as the wind caught that big chute, it lifted the back of the car right off the goddam ground. By the time it came down again, we were about 40 feet off-line to the left.

We might have gotten away with that if we were on a drag strip or an airport runway, but 190th Street didn't have a lot of runoff area. What it did have, right at the bottom of this hill, was a sprawling nursery full of trees of all sizes. We went tearing into that nursery, knocking over trees as we skidded along. And just before the car came to rest, it rolled over onto its side.

We crawled out of the rubble, dusted ourselves off, and pretty soon here came the Redondo Beach police. This one cop ran up and looked around. There were trees lying all over the place and a Chevrolet station wagon all bashed to hell with a parachute hanging off it. I'm quite sure he had never come across an accident scene like this one.

The cop paused and then said, "What the hell happened here?"

Mike Sarokin was a mouthy kid. He glanced around, stared up at the sky, and said, "You know, I don't think that airplane was high enough when they pushed us out."

Needless to say, the initial test of the first piece of Simpson safety equipment ended with Mike and me wearing metal bracelets and being chauffeured to the Redondo Beach jail.

Still, the experiment was a success because it taught me that you didn't need a very big parachute to slow down an automobile. After that I started making cross-form chutes that were only 10 or 12 feet across, and they worked just fine. In fact, that's essentially the same parachute design you see today on every form of drag car.

It was only a matter of weeks until we got the chutes to the point where we were selling them to racers. They caught on quickly because they were so much better than the old war-surplus chutes. Just like that, I was in business, operating as Simpson Drag Chutes. Mike Sarokin was my partner and our headquarters was the garage behind my house. Here we were, in this little shop, 22 feet wide and 20 feet deep, with my race car in one bay and a long sewing table in the other. That was our factory. I was 18 years old.

> **Tom McEwen:** *I remember Bill in that garage, sitting at a sewing machine. I didn't know if he was going to be successful or not, but I was hoping really hard that he was going to make enough money to keep going, because we needed a guy like him who was interested in safety.*

It doesn't sound like much of a start, but my life turned around thanks to that tiny shop. What it did, really, was give me a direction. Until I started the business, I had moved from job to job, doing anything I could to help fund my racing. For example, during the period when I made that first parachute, I was working in the sound department at MGM Studios. I had dated a girl whose father was a sound man, and he got me the gig. I'd go out to the movie locations and work as a cable boy, hauling rolls of wire and helping the guys who carried those big boom microphones. The job had its perks: The money was great, I got to see a lot of famous movie stars—all of 'em, it seemed, worked for MGM—and, best of all, I was a day laborer, meaning I only worked when I felt like working. Most weeks I worked one or two days in the sound department and spent the rest of my time sewing parachutes together.

Before long, the chute business became a genuine occupation and then an obsession. And it all started in that two-bay shop.

Want to know how big an impression that place left on me? Check this out: It was at 1760 Haynes Lane, Redondo Beach. I still remember the address. And check *this*: the Alberoni Sewing Machine Company still supplies us with our sewing machines.

As time rolled on, we expanded our product line and began to focus on the notion that all of the work being done to make race cars safer wasn't going to amount to much unless we made a driver's most immediate surroundings—his personal gear—safer too. We started making special gloves, seat belts, shoes and a few other items, all of which dealt with the fact that even the best car could hurt a guy if he wasn't adequately prepared for a fire or a crash. This extra production meant we outgrew the old Haynes Lane shop pretty quickly. We moved into a new shop in Harbor City that, at 3,000 square feet, seemed absolutely huge, but before long we outgrew that place too, and got an even bigger building in Torrance. Every time we came up with a new or better way to do things, we needed more room.

> **C.J. Hart:** *I'm sure Bill got some of his ideas from the fellows he raced with, but he also had a great brain of his own. He saw things that were needed, so he made them.*

One of our early items was a very crude driving suit for drag racers. It was a stiff, bulky uniform made out of an aluminized fabric. A lot of drag guys wore that suit, but it never had any potential beyond that market. It would have been impossible to wear one of those suits in, say, an Indy car because the damn things were so heavy that the driver would have died from dehydration in an hour. The only place where it made any sense to wear the thing was in a drag car, where you only put it on for a few minutes at a time.

In every other form of motorsports there was no such thing as an effective fire suit. Hell, at most of the short tracks the best drivers had never worn anything tougher than a cotton T-shirt and a good pair of dungarees. It wasn't surprising that a lot of very good race drivers paid a painful price for that.

> **Bobby Allison, 1983 NASCAR Winston Cup champion:** *In 1959 I ran a 500-lap Modified stock car race at Dixie Speedway, a quarter-mile asphalt oval outside Birmingham, Alabama. We knew that because of the length of the race we were going to have to refuel, but that was something we never did in the Modifieds, so we didn't have the proper equipment. My car was a '34 Chevy sedan with the gas tank behind the driver's seat, so I made a 10-gallon dump can and added a length of straight radiator hose, and got a couple of my friends to volunteer to reach through the side window and refuel the thing.*
>
> *Well, in the race, here I came into the pits. They were pouring the gas in, trying to hurry—and I was trying to hurry 'em, too—when they dropped the can. It rolled under the car and spilled gas everywhere, and naturally it caught fire. I was sitting in the car with a lot of heat on me, and it blistered my back and the backs of my arms pretty good.*
>
> *I was wearing a T-shirt put out by a little outfit in Birmingham that had a product called Vigorlube, an oil additive. The T-shirt said 'Save with Vigorlube,' and the part that said 'Save with' was kind of like a decal. Well, those words—Save with—were burned right into my back.*

Even at high-profile venues like Indianapolis, the hot ticket in personal safety gear was a flimsy cotton driving suit that the driver dipped into a mixture of Boraxo and water just before he put it on. To even call those outfits "firesuits" was ridiculous; they weren't anything close to that.

> **Parnelli Jones:** *We didn't have firesuits; we had uniforms.*

*They were little, thin suits that we had to dip in some kind of a solution, and it was a pain in the neck.*

**Bobby Allison:** *I had some of those early-style suits. Some of them you had to dip and some you didn't; I guess those had already been dipped for you. But, to tell you the truth, I wore those things mostly because I thought they looked pretty nice, not because I thought they would give me more protection.*

By the middle '60s it was clear that something was needed to offer drivers a better chance of surviving fires. When that something finally came along, it was a very big deal.

I had gotten to know Pete Conrad, the NASA astronaut who commanded the Apollo 12 mission, because he dabbled in road racing and had bought some of our products. One day Pete told me about a temperature-resistant material NASA was using to protect space capsules as they re-entered the earth's atmosphere. I asked Pete how I might be able to acquire some of that stuff, and he gave me the name of a person who could help me. It turned out to be available in fabric form, and I was excited the moment I saw it. It was not only fire-resistant, it was also everything our drag-suit material was not: It was light, it was flexible, and it breathed. It was clear to me immediately that I had found something that could revolutionize our sport.

The material was filament Nomex, and I was the first person to make a racing suit out of it. I took an old cotton driver's uniform and cut it apart; from there I made a pattern, put my ever-expanding sewing skills to work, and stitched up a suit out of Nomex.

I took that prototype suit to Roy Richter, who at that time owned several racing companies, including Cragar Industries and Bell Helmets. Back then, Bell was not exactly a competitor of mine. True, we were both in the safety business, but we made different things and I was pretty friendly with Roy because we were both from Southern California.

I said, "Roy, you need to see this." Then I wrapped some of that material around my arm, poured gasoline on it, and lit my arm on fire. The Nomex held up great. Roy was absolutely amazed.

He said, "Man, you have *got* to take this to Indianapolis."

In those days there were fires in all kinds of racing, but the biggest and baddest fires took place at Indy. Don't forget, this was 1967, only three years after Eddie Sachs and Dave MacDonald had burned to death in a horrible crash on the opening lap of the 500.

So I went to Indianapolis with a fellow named Ray Labely, who was Bell's director of marketing, and I showed that suit around. It was a hit. This was smack in the heyday of a big tire war between Goodyear and Firestone, and my first real score came when the bosses at Goodyear ordered suits for all their contract drivers. Then Firestone did the same thing, which gave us just about every driver in the 500.

I promised everybody they'd have their suits in time for the race, which was optimistic to say the least. Remember, our only uniform business to that point had been in drag racing, so I had only four or five ladies doing all of my sewing. Now here I was, holding rush orders for something like 60 or 70 of those Nomex suits. The only thing I could do was head home to California and help the ladies put those new suits together. It was a round-the-clock effort, certainly the first time the Simpson plant had operated with more than one shift.

We managed to fill all those orders and get them to Indy by the end of the month, but it was a monumental feat. TWA had a round-trip flight—Flight 183 going to Indianapolis International, Flight 184 back to LAX—and I made the trip several times that May, my suitcases stuffed full of those firesuits.

The tire companies were my first big customers and for that I've been forever grateful. But that Nomex suit was going to be a success anyway, no question. It was the latest, greatest thing in personal safety gear and every driver in the joint wanted one.

I had never seen, and to this day I have *still* never seen, a single piece of safety equipment that was instantly accepted the way the

Nomex fire suit was. Traditionally, race drivers were their own worst enemies when it came to safety; I mean, this was right around the same time when some guys began putting roll cages on sprint cars, and even though a cage sounds like an absolute no-brainer today, a lot of people were adamantly opposed to them in the late '60s. The bravest guys thought roll cages would somehow close the gap between them and everybody else.

Well, you didn't hear any of that macho bullshit when it came to firesuits. There isn't a driver alive, macho or not, who's not afraid of getting his ass burned up.

> ***A.J. Foyt, four-time Indianapolis 500 winner:*** *Fire was the big thing everybody was scared of, whether they were in Indy cars or stock cars or whatever. If you've ever been burned, like I got burned at Milwaukee and DuQuoin, you know why. Broken bones will heal; a burn will heal too, but while a burn is healing it hurts like hell.*

I believe the first two guys who tried the Nomex suits—actually wore 'em in their cars during Indy practice—were Foyt and Dan Gurney. That was a huge deal for me, because there weren't two bigger names in American racing at that point than A.J. and Dan. Come race day, there were something like 30 Nomex firesuits on the starting grid and they all said "Simpson" on the sleeve. I was proud of that. Still am.

Fortunately, 1967 was a pretty safe Indy 500 and nobody put one of our new suits to the test. Not that I was worried; I knew how the Nomex would hold up to flame because I had often repeated the same crude little burn test I had done for Roy Richter.

> ***Tom McEwen:*** *I used to go over to Simpson's place and watch him test-burn his uniforms with a torch, to see how long the different materials would hold up.*

Still, in the back of my mind I was a little bit anxious about how the suit would fare in a really bad blaze. Ironically enough, the first time one was really battle-tested the driver was my buddy and partner, Mike Sarokin. I can't remember exactly which drag strip we were at, but I do remember watching from the sidelines as Mike had a hellacious fire in his Top Fuel car. In the end he climbed out and he was just fine. The suit did its job spectacularly.

Actually, that fire helped us improve the suits because when I analyzed Mike's uniform I learned a lot about threads and closures and how they endured a fire of that magnitude. The whole thing taught me that it was a good idea, whenever possible, to look closely at any of our suits that were involved in serious fires. It was a way of making progress, of turning a negative into a positive.

> **Tom McEwen:** *Because I was involved with Simpson right from the beginning, I saw a lot of the things he did to improve his products. I mean, every time somebody got hurt, he would change this, change that. He was just relentless about this stuff.*

> **Gary Rovazzini, veteran Indy car mechanic:** *I remember being at Langhorne, Pennsylvania, one day when Sammy Sessions had a big crash in the first turn. The front of the car went underneath the guard rail and that pinned him in there; his legs and feet were trapped. In those days it didn't take much for those cars to catch fire, and this one did. The fuel was pouring out of the car and burning, and Sammy sat in that thing for a long time. I'm sure the majority of us standing there figured he was a goner. But he survived that fire and raced again, and Sammy was always quick to say that if he hadn't been wearing this brand-new suit Simpson had just given him, he wouldn't have made it through that fire.*

I've read in magazine articles that the fire suit was the biggest single advance in motorsports safety. I'm not sure about that, because there have certainly been a lot of important developments: Helmets have gotten better, roll-cage designs for all types of cars have been improved, tire technology has come a long way, composite construction has made Indy cars and formula cars safer, seats and restraint systems have evolved tremendously, and you cannot possibly overstate what the fuel cell did to enhance every driver's safety and peace of mind. But you'd have to rank the fire suit right up there, that's for sure, along with the gloves and shoes that complete any driver's personal safety gear.

And I'm very proud of the part I played in getting guys to start taking their personal safety gear seriously.

> **Bobby Allison:** *I was one of those guys who always figured that my most recent problem was going to be my last problem, and that anything bad that happened would happen to somebody else. Sure, I'd had a fire or two along the way, and we had seen some bad fires in stock car racing—Fireball Roberts was burned really badly at Charlotte [in 1964] and died from those burns later—but the really terrible fires always seemed to happen in Indy cars. So for a long time I simply operated under the idea that it couldn't happen to me. But little by little I began to see that you could have a bad fire even in a fully enclosed stock car, and that a good protective uniform—a real fire suit—could definitely be a big help. And I went from a very casual attitude about this to being pretty darned particular: I had to have a suit that fit me just right and was made from whatever was the best material at the time.*

> **Don Prudhomme:** *It took me a long time, too long, to start paying attention to safety equipment. When you're young and you start racing, you'd drive one of those things naked if you had to. But then something happened in the late*

*'60s that changed all that for me. There was a guy by the name of John Mulligan, who was a good friend of mine and McEwen's. We were at the U.S. Nationals, in Indianapolis, and John had a tremendous fire at the end of the quarter-mile. In those days in drag racing, we didn't lose a lot of drivers from burns; guys died in crashes, but not so much in fires. So we didn't know a lot about burns and, truthfully, neither did the doctors. Well, lo and behold, a few weeks later John died from those burns, which just shocked us all.*

*Tom McEwen: After Mulligan got burned, I pulled both my cars out of the race and went to the hospital. It was just a bad deal. And when he died we all really started looking harder at this safety stuff.*

*Don Prudhomme: From that point on, I think all of us in drag racing started turning up the heat to change things. And Bill Simpson, in my opinion, was the guy responsible for us getting better gloves and better suits and better underwear.*

All of these safety improvements I've mentioned had their roots in a period of roughly 10 years, from the middle 1960s to the mid-'70s, and that's pretty amazing to think about. In that time the bar for driver safety in all forms of motorsports was raised maybe 500 percent. That level of improvement has never been duplicated; today, any gains we can make are incremental.

Unfortunately, the sport still wasn't 100 percent safe. By its nature it can't be. That point had been drilled into me right from the very beginning, and it was driven home again one night in 1968, when Mike Sarokin was killed at Orange County. He was a great driver in a great car and he was wearing the very best safety equipment available, but none of that could save him. The car's rear end broke out of its mounts—one of those things that happened occasionally as dragsters evolved—and thrashed around violently. It tore Mike all to hell.

You'd think that by then I would have gotten used to losing my buddies, but I wasn't. Losing Mike Sarokin devastated me.

By that time I'd gotten away from drag racing a bit because the business kept pulling me elsewhere. I had quit driving drag cars on a regular basis in '64, but I stayed in the sport as a team owner for a few years. Mike had driven for me, as had Paul Sutherland. But Mike's death made it hard to hang around the drag strips. I got out of drag racing altogether, as a participant, in 1970.

Understand this: I didn't leave because I didn't like the sport anymore. I never really had a single crowning moment as a drag-race driver, but I've always loved drag racing and I still do. After all, drag racing is what got me into this game. And I had come to love its crazy little rivalries—like the way the West Coast guys, the Midwest guys and the East Coast guys all thought they were the toughest SOBs in the game. If you were from California, you couldn't tolerate a Chicago guy or an East Coast guy accomplishing anything first. That's why as soon as word got out that somebody had broken a magical elapsed-time barrier in one part of the country, the drag racers who lived elsewhere were quick to respond that one of their guys had done exactly the same thing.

"You saw a 7.8? Hey, we just had one here, too!"

Look it up: On both coasts and in Middle America, everybody broke the seven-second quarter-mile barrier on the same weekend. Later on, everybody dipped into the sixes on the same weekend. How can you not love a sport made up of guys who are that competitive?

(By the way, there is still some dispute over who was the first guy to run 200 miles per hour in a Top Fuel car. Chris Karamesines generally gets the credit, but because of all the fibbing that went on back then, there are those who are a bit skeptical about this. Me, I'll stick with the Greek. He's my friend and that's good enough for me.)

No, I didn't gradually go sour on drag racing. I guess maybe I was just starting to feel a little stale. I've never been a person who could remain static for very long; I've got to keep moving. I had been in drag racing for something like 15 years by then, and I was simply ready for new challenges.

Besides, there's something to be said about going out on a high note, and I sure did that in drag racing. The last car I owned was a Top Fueler called the Simpson Skyjacker, and Norm "The Rocket" Wilcox drove it. We ran it eight times and won eight times. I figured that was a pretty good way to exit.

# 3

# On the Gas

By 1970, when I sold off the last of my drag equipment, the whole focus of my racing life had changed. That was a direct by-product of the business taking off; the more exposure I got to other forms of motorsports, the more fascinated with them I became.

That was particularly true when it came to one very special race track: the Indianapolis Motor Speedway.

I had fallen in love with Indy the moment I walked into the joint back in 1967. I was consumed by the history, by the tradition, by the sheer size of the 500. The teams were there for most of the month of May. Hell, just *qualifying* for the 500 took two weekends. The opening Saturday of time trials was called Pole Day and the final Sunday of qualifying was called Bump Day. At Indianapolis they got bigger crowds on Pole Day and Bump Day than most tracks did on race day.

The fact that the greatest drivers in the world treated Indy with reverence made me treat it that way too. I liked the way racers all over the globe referred to it as simply "the Speedway." To me that just underscored the importance of the place.

The very first time I walked through Gasoline Alley, the Indianapolis garage area, I promised myself that I would be back there one day as a driver entered in the 500. I wasn't sure exactly how I was going to do that, but I had a hunch.

A couple of years prior to '67 I had gotten involved in road racing, competing in several different formula-car classes with the Sports Car Club of America. It seemed to me that the formula cars might help me get to Indianapolis because they were somewhat similar to Indy cars; they were rear-engine machines with independent suspensions, just like the cars that had blown the old roadsters out of Indianapolis in the mid-'60s.

If nothing else, the SCCA's formula cars were a hell of a lot closer to Indy cars than the dragsters I had been driving.

Actually, my SCCA involvement had a strange origin. Paul Sutherland and I had been hauling all over the country, match-racing our dragster, and one day we were up in Wisconsin. Well, it just so happened that somebody—I can't remember who—was testing an Indy car at Milwaukee. Paul and I went over there to watch and we were awed by that car's speed and handling.

Later, Sutherland said, "You know, I'd really like to try driving one of those things."

I said, "Me too."

Paul knew about a road-racing school in Willow Springs, California, so we went up there and signed on. Today it's the Jim Russell School, an institution with a great international reputation, but back then it was just a small-time deal run by a little Englishman named Wally. He put us in a couple of formula cars and instructed us to watch our speed by keeping an eye on the tachometer and staying under 4,000 RPM.

What that showed me was that Wally wasn't a very good judge of character. It should have been clear that a couple of drag-racing refugees like us weren't going to be very good at following orders. Right away we began running wide open, and it was only a matter of time before one of us wrecked. Paul beat me to it. He slid off turn one and flipped his car upside-down. That was the end of the class, at least for us, because Wally threw us out of his school.

But we'd had some fun in our short time with Wally, enough for me to look further into this road-racing deal. It had two big advantages on drag racing, I figured: All the right and left turns made it more challenging, from a driver's point of view; and you weren't blowing up your stuff constantly and having to rebuild engines all the time.

I went out and bought myself a little Brabham and eased myself into road racing. I don't even remember what class I raced in, but I had a lot of success with that car. We won fairly often. That began the process of moving through the various formula classes, right up through Formula Continental—a class for four-cylinder overhead-cam Ford engines and cars similar to Super Vees—and then Formula 5000.

Right from the start I had fun in road racing, mostly because we were competitive wherever we went. I won at Willow Springs and at Riverside, California, one of the great American road circuits. I won at Castle Rock, outside Denver. We even raced in the streets of Tijuana, and I won there.

At the time, winning those races gave me a great sense of accomplishment. Looking back, it probably wasn't that big a deal. The plain truth is that I wasn't racing against a very tough field. The SCCA had always been primarily an amateur club and therefore most of its entrants were hobby racers, just rich guys out to thrill themselves on the weekends.

That's not to say there weren't a few really good race drivers in the SCCA. Some of them still stand out in my mind: There was Dr. Lou Sell, a dentist who was later badly burned in a crash at Riverside; there was a kid out of Oregon named Love who was a bullet, just blindingly fast; there was David Webster, another dentist, who was always quick; and there were Joe Alves and Skeeter McItrick, two more really good racers.

Those were the guys I usually ran with. No matter how many cars showed up, when the green flag waved it was always the same handful of us who took off and ran for the win. And we fought hard for it, because we saw ourselves as serious racers.

The hobbyists never knew exactly what to make of guys like us. We would drive the hell out of our cars, and when you do that, sometimes you crash. I'd be out there, running on the ragged edge, and maybe I'd slide into a barrier and knock a wheel off. To a lot of those SCCA regulars, the idea of crashing like that was terrible. It didn't matter to them that we were often several seconds per lap faster than they were; it just appalled them that we abused our cars that way.

This was how they approached a race: You showed up with your shiny car, ran the event, then took the car home and washed it off so it'd be nice and shiny again for the next week. To them a race wasn't a race at all; it was an occasion to socialize.

Not surprisingly, I didn't fit in very well with that crowd, but it wasn't anything personal. All I cared about was learning how to make my car work better and how to drive it faster. Hanging out with a bunch of rich dudes didn't interest me. To tell you the truth, they probably weren't interested in hanging out with me, either.

The time I spent in SCCA did a lot to build my confidence. It showed me that when things were right, I was capable of driving pretty well. I was aware that if I had been racing against fields that included more top-class drivers, I would have had a harder struggle, but that only increased my desire to get better.

In 1968, after about four seasons in SCCA, I wanted to see just how good I had gotten. The final Indy car race of the season was coming up on the first weekend in December, at Riverside, and I decided to enter. I didn't know if I was ready or not; I wasn't dominating my SCCA class by any stretch of the imagination and I was still crashing too much. But I was winning races and running regularly in the top four or five, and I had come to realize that if I stuck around SCCA much longer, I'd probably be there forever. And that wasn't what I wanted. I wanted to go to Indianapolis. So I got my hands on a used Indy car and started to get it ready.

> *Larry Burton, veteran Indy car mechanic: I began working with Bill when he got his first Indy car, which was a Howard Gilbert Cheetah. What it was, really, was a copy of a Brabham powered by a Chevy engine. We put that thing together right in the same shop in Torrance where Simpson made his firesuits and parachutes. He cleared out a spot in the back corner, moved the race car in, and put up a parti-*

*tion between us and the sewing machines. The girls who*
*worked on the sewing machines used to bring us our lunch.*

I filled out an entry blank for the Riverside race and mailed it to the United States Auto Club, which at the time was the governing body in Indy car racing. That got my name printed in the pre-race publicity stories because I was the latest outsider making his way into the Indy car ranks. Well, that didn't sit too well with the Sports Car Club of America. They sent me a letter explaining that if I ran with USAC, I would lose my SCCA license. This was typical of the bullshit all the big sanctioning bodies used to put their drivers through; their aim was to keep you in line by strong-arming you. But I told everybody who would listen, "Screw them. I'm going to race where I want to race, not where they tell me I can race."

Some people suggested that I should try to smooth things over with the SCCA, but I didn't see any sense in that. I mean, when you get a letter like that—a letter that is a point-blank threat to kick your ass out of the organization—you have to sit down and ask yourself if you really want to be part of that organization in the first place. And this time, I didn't. So I went to Riverside.

Of course, I discovered that USAC wasn't above using its own strong-arm tactics. Harry McQuinn was the chief steward of the Indy car series, and he was a pretty imposing guy. He drove me around the track in the pace car, making a point to tell me that I was no Al Unser, that I was no A.J. Foyt. Hell, I knew that. But when McQuinn said, "We're going to watch you very closely and if you make one wrong move you won't be welcomed back," he got my attention.

### Johnny Rutherford, three-time Indy 500 winner:
*Those USAC officials were tough, and that stemmed from the education they got from some of the old AAA officials. In the days before USAC, AAA sanctioned Indianapolis and they always let you know who was in charge. You did what they told you to do, and it was like, "If you screw up, kid, you're gone."*

> *I can remember, for example, absolutely fearing Harlan Fen-*
> *gler, the old chief steward at Indianapolis. In my rookie year*
> *at the Speedway I spun in the first turn during the final*
> *phase of my driver's test and I thought, That's it. I'm done.*
> *I'm out of here. Luckily, they didn't chase me away. But they*
> *were very tough on rookie drivers in those days.*

All these years later, I don't remember many details about how that Riverside weekend unfolded. I guess it was so exciting for me just to be there that I didn't absorb a lot of it. The record book shows me starting the race in 30th, but there's more to the story than that. Technically, I missed the show—our old car was heavy and underpowered—but when another guy failed to start, I got in as first alternate.

I do remember the race itself, a 300-miler, being a whole lot more intense than any race I'd ever driven before. Unlike the SCCA guys I had run against, the entire field at Riverside was made up of hard-core racers, which turned every pass into a real dogfight.

Unfortunately, the fun ended too quickly. My tired old car gave out early and I finished a miserable 27th. Still, that Riverside event made me more determined than ever to improve as a driver. I'd had a taste of racing at the top level, and I wanted more.

USAC had a fair number of road races in that period, and over the next year I ran most of them. Considering our equipment and the fact that I usually had only a couple of steady helpers, we did all right. We finished eighth at Indianapolis Raceway Park, seventh at Brainerd, Wisconsin. And I started mixing in a few oval-track events. We ran the old one-mile track in Hanford, California, along with Milwaukee and Phoenix.

All through 1969 I could tell I was getting better. By the time we got back to Riverside, for the season finale, I had plenty of Indy car miles under my belt and my confidence had grown. I think it showed in my driving. That Sunday I finished eighth. It was my third top-ten finish of the year.

I remember something funny that happened about two-thirds of the way through that Riverside race in '69: I needed a new pair of goggles, which happens occasionally; once you get enough oil and other junk smeared on 'em, they're useless. During my last pit stop I signaled to my guys that I needed a new pair, then I tore off the old goggles and threw 'em out of the car. The problem was, my eyeglasses went with them. I didn't realize this until I pulled out of the pits to rejoin the race and everything looked blurry. In those days I needed glasses to see any real distance. This got my attention because Riverside was a really fast road course, not the kind of place you'd want to drive while squinting. I thought about making an extra pit stop, but decided to go ahead and run the rest of the race.

> **Larry Burton:** *Driving without his glasses, I think he hit every car on the track before the end of the day.*

I thought that eighth-place finish was pretty respectable for a guy driving half-blind. It was also respectable in light of the caliber of the competition. So many of the stars of that era—Foyt, Mario Andretti, Al and Bobby Unser, Rutherford—were heroes of mine, and it was pretty cool to have spent almost a full season running against them. That's not to say it was easy; those guys were awfully intimidating to a young driver just coming along. You understood very quickly that no matter what you had done before in other forms of racing, you were in their domain now.

> **Bill Vukovich Jr., former Indy car driver:** *Don't forget, Simpson came out of road racing. He had done some drag racing first, but right before he came to Indy cars he had been a road racer. Well, in those days we looked at road racers as guys who had to squat to pee.*

> **Johnny Rutherford:** *I don't think any of us veterans intentionally intimidated anybody. I think that any intimidation*

*took place on the race track itself. You'd catch a young kid and pass him and just keep on going, and that can bother a guy who doesn't have a lot of experience. When I was a rookie, guys like Rodger Ward and Jim Rathmann and Troy Ruttman would drive off and just leave me, and I'd be sitting there saying, "How in the hell can they go so fast?"*

I had a very healthy respect for my competition, but at the same time I knew that if I was going to get anyplace, I was going to have to stand up for myself. The '69 season toughened me up that way. At Riverside Gordon Johncock and I were racing for position. He wasn't the big name he became later on, when he won Indy in 1973 and '82, but Gordy was certainly an established guy. Anyway, he made an inside move on me heading into turn one. I didn't think he was far enough alongside me, so I took my normal line into the corner and chopped him a little bit. Our two cars came together and Johncock spun. Well, he was pretty pissed off; I guess he figured I was supposed to move over for him. He complained to me after the race and I said, "Hey, I was ahead of you. It's just as much my race track as it is yours, and you ain't going to intimidate me."

And, really, most of them *didn't* intimidate me anymore, at least on road courses. I saw that I could hold my own against the majority of the USAC regulars when we went road racing. I remember clearly an incident at Riverside when I came up behind Sam Sessions during practice. I followed him around for a while and realized he was an accident waiting to happen. Now, Sessions was a great oval-tracker who came to Indy cars from the supermodified wars, so he was a solid racer; he just happened to be clueless about road racing because of his background.

When we got back to the pits I said, "Hey, Sammy, if you'll follow me I'll show you how to get around this place." We went out together in the next practice and I helped him cut his lap time by a fair amount.

That worked the other way around, too. The first time I ever ran an oval track, which was at Phoenix, I crashed. And I had a lot of very good oval racers—Bill Vukovich Jr., Jim Malloy, Art Pollard and, yes, Sam Sessions—tell me, "Man, you can't drive this place like it's a road course. You'll just keep getting into trouble."

They were right, because I was as clueless on that oval as Sessions had been on a road course.

> **Bill Vukovich Jr.:** *The road-race guys used to use the brakes a lot, for some reason. I'm sure this had been instilled in them by having to run into very tight, slow corners. On the ovals we used the brakes a bit, but not like those guys did; they would back off real early to get on the brakes, and you can't drive an oval that way.*

The more ovals I ran, the better I got. At Milwaukee in 1970 I finished sixth, so I knew I was going in the right direction.

I was logging laps whenever and wherever I could. I even went to Australia and New Zealand in the winter of 1969 and 70, to run in the old Tasman Series for Formula 5000 and Indy-type cars.

The Tasman was an incredibly competitive bunch of races. There was nothing else going on in the motor-racing world at that time of the year, so all kinds of great drivers—Formula One guys, Indy car guys, sports car guys, you name it—would show up. You could never duplicate that series today, because the top F1 and Indy car guys are too busy and too rich to give a damn about a midwinter series on the other side of the world, but 30 years ago it was a real happening.

We went there with a Gurney Eagle that belonged to John Crean, who owned Fleetwood Homes, and the actor James Garner. It was a good little team, with Larry Burton as crew chief. We squeaked into the top five in the final standings, which I thought was excellent.

> **Larry Burton:** *Our Eagle had originally been built for an American Motors V-8, but we converted it to run a Chevy. It was a little heavy and a little bit outclassed by most of the*

*other cars down there; I mean, we were running against Lo-*
*tuses and Ferraris and some pretty good teams. But Bill gave*
*that thing a hell of a ride.*

I did all of these things simply to gear myself up for Indianapolis. The Speedway had become the Holy Grail for me, and I was inching toward the 500 one race at a time.

# 4

# Tough Times in the Big Leagues

By 1970 I figured I was ready. The Indianapolis 500 is unique in that before you're even allowed to make a qualifying attempt, you have to pass through a program called Rookie Orientation. It's really a driving test supervised by race officials and a hand-picked group of Indy veterans. You'd better have your act together when you take that test; plenty of drivers have flunked Rookie Orientation, for one reason or another, and never gotten another crack at the 500.

I covered my bases by putting together a deal to do my rookie test in a car owned by Bob Wilke and maintained by A.J. Watson, one of the greatest mechanics ever to lay his hands on a race car. It was an honor for me just to sit in a car Watson had worked on, and he was also the perfect guy to coach a driver through a rookie test because he was so calm and casual about things. Thanks to Wilke and Watson, I got through the test without a hitch.

I entered the race in a car owned by Myron Caves and wrenched by Bob Higman, but we didn't get to run the 500. In fact we never made an official qualifying attempt because everything went wrong. On the final Sunday of qualifying, a line came loose from the oil pressure gauge and started spraying hot oil into my lap, which definitely got my attention. I pulled down into the grass in turn one and jumped out, a little bit burned but otherwise OK. But when they took me into the infield hospital for the mandatory check-up, the medics decided I shouldn't run anymore that day, and that was that.

Still, May of 1970 was pretty memorable because of something that happened in Gasoline Alley. I had been around Indy cars for a couple of seasons by then and I'd say I was accepted by 50 or 60 percent of the drivers. The trouble was, the remaining ones who did *not* accept me were some of the biggest names in the sport. It was all the old-line hard cases: Foyt, Bobby Unser, guys like that. I'm sure they respected the work I had done on the safety front, but they didn't want to welcome Bill Simpson the race driver into their little clique. I had long hair and a mustache, and to them I was just a wise-ass kid from California.

> ### John Martin, former Indy car driver and owner:
> *Bill was always the rebel. Always late for meetings, always had the long hair, sometimes had a beard. He was just a little bit different.*

Anyway, a whole gang of them showed up one day at the door of my garage. One of them was holding a pair of scissors and they announced that they were going to give me a proper haircut. Well, I figured that if they had scissors, I needed something on my side, too. I picked up a wheel hammer and said, "You sonsabitches are not cutting my hair, and that's the end of that." There was a brief standoff, but within a few minutes everybody seemed to decide that maybe I didn't need a haircut right at that moment.

> ### A.J. Foyt: *I'm quite sure that if they'd really wanted to cut his hair, they could have, because Simpson wasn't that bad. He wasn't that tough.*

They never really bothered me again, but for a long time I didn't get along well with that crowd. I guess it was simply a clash of cultures.

The next few years were really frustrating for me. I had gotten a taste of the Speedway and I wanted more than ever to be a part of

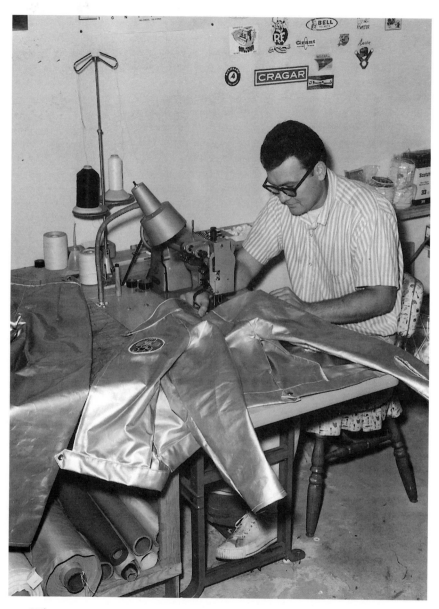

When you start out small, like I did, you can't be afraid of hard work. This is me back in, oh, probably 1962, in my little garage on Haynes Lane in Redondo Beach, California. I'm sewing together an aluminized driving suit, the kind all the drag racers used in those days. You can see how heavy, bulky and uncomfortable those things were. (*Bill Simpson Collection*)

Me again, helping with parachute production. I'm not sure whose chute this was, but it's pretty obvious he was sponsored by Bardahl. In the background you can see our entire work force: two ladies from the neighborhood.
(*Bill Simpson Collection*)

ABOVE: These days our seatbelt assembly process is pretty complicated and mostly automated. Back in the early '60s, though, the sewing was done by hand. When racers started taking safety more seriously and orders began to flow in, these ladies and their sewing machines got very busy. (*Bill Simpson Collection*)

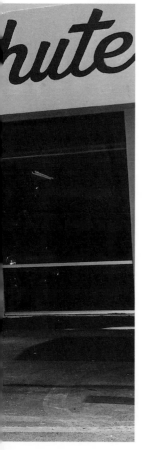

LEFT: Man, I'm looking pretty big-time here. I'm outside my storefront, in Harbor City, California, fitting a chute to my dragster. This location was my first move out of my little garage, and it was a big step up for the company. (*Bill Simpson Collection*)

ABOVE: This is a publicity shot we set up when I introduced the "pure air" race suit. In the 1960s dragster and Funny Car drivers sat right behind the engine, with little or nothing to block fumes or flames or whatever else the motor belched up, so I put together a fire mask with a built-in respirator. That's my first wife, Janice, watching me hand the first pure-air suit to McEwen. And check out Mongoose's street car: He was sponsored by the Plymouth Dealers of Southern California, so he rode around Los Angeles in that thing. (*Bill Simpson Collection*)

RIGHT: This is kind of a rare photo—rare because during this period, the 1960s, I didn't have much leisure time. But that's Janice and me with our sons, Dave and Jeff, doing a little surf-casting. It looks like we're all sporting the latest Simpson Drag Chutes apparel. (*Bill Simpson Collection*)

# ChampCar Team Member for a Weekend Sweepstakes

# OFFICIAL ENTRY FORM

**ENTER TO WIN!**

☐ **YES!** Enter my name in the Team Member for a Weekend Sweepstakes Giveaway and also enter (or extend) my 1 year (6 issues) subscription to *Champ Car* for only $19.97.

☐ **NO,** I don't wish to subscribe at this time, but please enter my name in the Sweepstakes.

Name _____ e-mail Address _____

Address _____ City _____ State _____ Zip _____

9LDA

**ENTER TO WIN!**

# Champ Car™

PO BOX 18449
ANAHEIM CA 92817-9930

Here I am with Tom "Mongoose" McEwen, back when we were both skinny. He's checking out a new drag parachute shortly after we introduced the cross-form canopy. That was a pretty innovative product, and the top drag guys, like McEwen, all lined up to buy one. (*Bill Simpson Collection*)

OPPOSITE: Before we introduced the Nomex firesuit in 1967, the standard uniform for a race driver was what you see Jim Hurtubise wearing here, at Indianapolis in 1960—just a cotton suit dipped in a chemical solution to make it more fire-resistant. That's Eddie Sachs, another Indy legend, holding the microphone. Jim had just broken Eddie's track record, so Eddie, always a joker, decided that the old record holder ought to interview the new one. It was Eddie's death, in the '64 Indy 500, that help build the demand for safer driving gear. (*Photo courtesy Indianapolis Motor Speedway*)

BELOW: If you were wearing one of the old cotton driving uniforms, you didn't stick around long once a fire broke out. This is my buddy Parnelli Jones bailing out of his moving car on pit road at Indianapolis in 1964 after the fuel tank blew up. You can't see the fire, because methanol burns with an invisible flame, but you can see some unburned fuel trailing the car, and the big hole at the top of the tank, just behind the roll bar, where the filler valve was blown away. (*Photo courtesy Indianapolis Motor Speedway*)

What a difference a good suit makes! Instead of bailing out at speed, like Parnelli had done in '64, Jim McElreath was able to stop his burning car and climb out with relative ease at the 1969 Indy 500, despite having a fairly nasty fire on board. (*Photo courtesy Indianapolis Motor Speedway*)

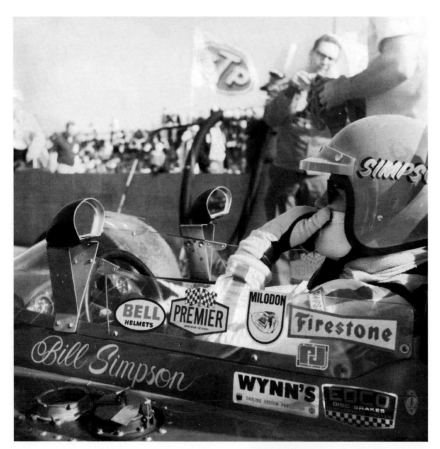

ABOVE: This shot might be a collector's item—not because it's from one of my very first Indy car events but because of the Bell Helmets decal on my car. In those days, my product line hadn't yet expanded to include headgear. (*Bill Simpson Collection*)

RIGHT: In 1970 I showed up at Indianapolis for the first time as a driver, with a car owned by Myron Caves. Unfortunately we had all kinds of problems, culminating in a broken oil line that sprayed hot oil into my lap on the final day of qualifying, and we didn't make the cut. (*Photo courtesy Indianapolis Motor Speedway*)

BELOW: You can tell by the number of guys working on my car that my 1970 Indy effort was kind of a low-dollar operation. A lot of guys used to go to the Speedway on shoestring budgets, and we all found out that you can quickly nickel-and-dime yourself right out of that race. (*John Mahoney photo*)

ABOVE: At Indy in 1970, when I was explaining the improvements in our latest suit, I said, "Look, I'll just put one on and you guys can light me on fire." A bunch of drivers, mechanics, and onlookers marched down to the infield inside turn one. They poured the gasoline and then George Snider tossed the match. The suit held up fine. One driver looking on was Sammy Sessions, who later credited a Simpson suit for saving his butt when he was trapped in his burning car in a crash at Langhorne, Pennsylvania. Note the comedian roasting a hot dog. (*Photo courtesy Indianapolis Motor Speedway*)

In the early 1970s the USAC Indy car circuit included several road courses. I had come from an SCCA formula-car background, so in those Indy car road races I always ran pretty well, considering our equipment and the fact that I usually had only a couple of steady helpers. This shot was taken at Indianapolis Raceway Park, where I had an eighth-place finish. You can tell this is an old photo because I'm wearing a Bell Helmets patch! I hadn't yet gone into the headgear business (*John Mahoney photo*)

ABOVE: In 1971 it looked like I was a cinch to qualify for my first Indianapolis 500. Then, on the last corner of my final time-trial lap, my only engine exploded. I was able to coast across the line, but I ended up missing the starting field by something like two-tenths of a second. If that damned engine had only lived for another quarter-mile. . . . (*Bill Simpson Collection*)

Check out the hot-shot Indy car racer. This is from 1971, in my struggling owner/driver phase. I was always able to find modest backing—in this case from Wynn's—but the bulk of the money came right out of my pocket, which wasn't very deep in those days. You can also see the shaggy hair and mustache that set me apart from most of the clean-cut Indy car guys back then.
(*Bill Simpson Collection*)

After a driver completes his qualifying run at Indianapolis, they stop him on pit road for a traditional series of photos. This picture is from 1971, the year we blew the engine just at the end of our time-trial. From left to right, that's Cliff Haverson, Firestone's Rodger Ward Jr., Ted Swiontek, Gary Rovazzini, and me. We're smiling because at that moment it looked like we might make the line-up despite the trouble. Unfortunately, we were wrong. (*Photo courtesy Indianapolis Motor Speedway*)

In 1973 I drove this car, the Norton Spirit, for Rolla Vollstedt. Rolla's car was a copy of a McLaren, which was one of the hot designs back then, but it sure didn't run like a McLaren. In fact, I had one of the worst crashes of my life in this car at Indy that May. (*Bill Simpson Collection*)

Here's why the clean-cut, old-guard Indy car establishment didn't take to me right away. Here's how I looked at Indy in 1972—shaggy hair, mustache and all. This was pretty much the height of my rebellious phase. (*John Mahoney photo*)

In the early 1970s wings were the hot new aerodynamic trick in Indy cars, and they made the older equipment instant antiques. We tried just to add wings to our existing cars, but we couldn't keep up with the latest McLarens and Eagles, which had been designed for those big wings. That's Willie Dixon, a legendary USAC mechanic who worked on everything from Indy cars to sprinters, checking out my car during practice at the Speedway. (*John Mahoney photo*)

the 500, but I had all kinds of trouble there. I was trying to be a driver and a car owner both, and I had no business doing that because I didn't have the money it took.

> **Gary Rovazzini:** *When I worked with Bill, in the early '70s, we had a budget of next to nothing. I remember working on the car day and night, and then hauling it across the country. We had to sleep in the truck a lot of times, just because we didn't have the money for hotel rooms. I'll tell you how bad it was: At Indianapolis companies would give away parts—nuts, bolts, hose clamps, all kinds of things—and we couldn't wait until May just so we could get rid of all our old parts and put on this new stuff! We'd change every nut and bolt on the car at Indy, just because we got this new stuff free.*

When May rolled around I'd show up at the Speedway with just one car and just one engine and pray that something good would happen. Of course it never did.

In 1971 I came out of turn four on the final lap of my qualifying attempt and my only engine exploded. I ended up missing the field by something like two-tenths of a second, so I would have been a cinch to make the 500 if that goddam engine had only lived for another quarter-mile. But things like that happen when you try to run Indianapolis on a shoestring.

To tell you the truth, I ran *everywhere* on a shoestring. One year, back when Indy cars raced at the old Texas World Speedway, I blew my tired old Offenhauser engine so badly that the block split in half and dumped its insides all over the track. That night I was in the bar at the Holiday Inn, licking my wounds, and Roger Penske walked in. He asked me if I was going to be able to get my car running and I told him I didn't have a spare engine.

Roger said, "Tell you what I'll do. I've got a brand-new Offy with me. I'll flip you double or nothing for it."

At the time, a new Offenhauser went for about $15,000, which was a ton of money in those days, and I was looking at a chance to get one free if I won the coin toss. If I lost, I was going to owe Roger Penske $30,000, but at least I'd have myself a fresh engine.

The commonsense thing for a pauper like me would have been to cut my losses, walk straight out of that bar and go to bed. But common sense goes right out the window when you dangle a new engine in front of a hungry race driver.

I said, "Flip the coin."

He did. I called heads, and I lost.

It took me a year to pay Penske his 30 grand. But I'll tell you what, that was one honkin' Offy engine I got. It put me in the race that Sunday at Texas, so I figured it was worth it.

Even back then, in the early '70s, Penske was one of the sport's most controversial team owners. He was a wealthy guy and his outfit was among the first of Indy car racing's real "superteams." At the top of the heap you had Roger's team, the Vel's/Parnelli Jones team, Dan Gurney's team, Team McLaren, Pat Patrick's team and Foyt's team. The rest of us, on the other hand, were so broke that we shouldn't even have dreamed of owning Indy cars. We had the money it took to *own* them, but we didn't necessarily have the money it took to *race* 'em.

To put all this in perspective using, say, 1972 or '73 numbers, you could buy a pretty complete Eagle from Gurney's shop for $24,000. All you had to do was plug in an engine and you could go racing. So, tacking on another 15 grand for an Offy and, say, another $10,000 for incidentals, you could call yourself an Indy car owner for less than $50,000, which wasn't an extravagant sum of money even then. The problem was, then you had to actually race the thing—you had to buy wheels and tires, you had to pay for engine overhauls, you had to replace any suspension pieces you might have bent if you brushed the wall. Like I said, owning a car is one thing and racing it is another.

The low-buck teams showed up at the Speedway each May with maybe $25,000 in sponsorship to get them through the month. I don't know what Penske was spending, but any time he needed something, money wasn't a factor; he just went and got it. If you told me Roger's Indy budget alone was a half-million dollars, I'd say you were in the ballpark.

My budget for an entire season back then never went over $60,000 to $70,000 because the money just wasn't there. Penske, McLaren, and the bigger outfits were spending a million-plus and not even feeling the pinch.

This scenario often left the rich guys on one side of the fence and the rest of us on the other. Once it almost led to a fight between Penske and me at Indianapolis.

The whole thing was about the pros and cons of wings, which were the hot new aerodynamic trick in Indy cars and were making the older cars, mine included, into instant antiques. Mark Donohue was driving Penske's car, the latest and greatest McLaren, and it had a wing on it. Well, a bunch of guys were discussing wings and Roger put in his opinion, which was different from mine. So I did what I always did in situations like that in those days: I got right in Penske's face. I said, "Screw you, man. You ought to think about the rest of us once in a while. All this trick shit is going to put us right out of business." I was pretty hot, mad enough to punch someone, and it showed.

> **Roger Penske, 10-time Indianapolis 500-winning car owner:** *Simpson and I nearly got in a fight, right there at the Speedway. Hell, he was grabbing me by the shirt and vice-versa.*

Looking back, I know I was way out of line. Roger was entitled to his opinion, just like I was entitled to mine. Besides, I was the one who chose to bring my low-dollar ride to Indy; Penske didn't make me do that. If I couldn't stand the heat in the kitchen, I shouldn't have volunteered to be the cook.

A couple years later, when our relationship was still a bit unsettled, Penske said to me, "I like you, Simpson. You're the only guy who ever came close to punching me out." We had a good laugh over that one.

> *Roger Penske: You know, in racing you're going to have tempers flaring sometimes. But Bill was a guy who became my friend. Whatever happened that day at Indianapolis might have been a big deal at the time, but it certainly means nothing today.*

Roger is a guy who has put his heart and his soul, not just his money, into this sport, and there is nobody in the entire world of motorsports whom I respect more than I respect Roger Penske. But that one day at Indy we were pretty far apart and it almost got out of hand. Being broke will do that.

I did the best I could, but I could never afford to run the entire USAC circuit. I concentrated on the road courses and on the oval tracks I liked: Trenton, Milwaukee, Phoenix, Ontario. When things were right, we were capable of doing well. One day we were at Trenton, where we had qualified 10th with a stock-block Chevrolet engine against everybody else's expensive Offies. I was standing beside my mechanic, Jim Ward, as the national anthem was played. Jim looked up and down the grid, then nodded at our car and said, "If I was one of these guys who got out-qualified by this piece of shit, I'd hang myself from that flagpole." But, as usual, the last joke was on us that day; we were running well when a rocker arm broke.

By the end of 1972 I'd had enough of all this frustration. I had been around Indy car racing for a few years by then and I had a clear view of reality. It didn't take a genius to see that if you didn't have your act together you weren't going anywhere at this level of the sport. And my act was just about the exact opposite of together.

> *Gary Rovazzini: One day Bill and I and Larry Burton pulled out of Indianapolis heading for Trenton. We were al-*

*most there when one of the trailer tires went flat. Bill and I took that tire and wheel, hitchhiked into town, and found the local Firestone dealer. We had no money to speak of; we had come all that way just working off our credit cards to buy gas. There was no way we could afford even one trailer tire. But we were one of Firestone's Indy car teams, so we asked the dealer to call Firestone in Akron. We had to wait three or four hours, but Akron finally called back and told the dealer it was OK to give us this trailer tire.*

**Tom Smith, veteran Indy car mechanic:** *When I was with Bill we never had much to work with. It was always a case where, with a little bit of ingenuity and a lot of work, we'd do all right—but it was a struggle. We were at Ontario in '72 and that happened to be the race where Jerry Grant became the first man to qualify an Indy car at over 200 miles per hour. I saw Jerry on pit road and I congratulated him. He said, "Hell, if anybody deserves congratulations, you guys do, for getting that shitbox of yours into the race."*

All the while, my safety business was growing. I found myself spending half my time looking after the business and the other half messing around with my race cars, which, to be honest, were nothing but junk. Something had to give.

I decided I had to sell off my racing equipment and find a ride with another team. The way I figured it, even if I ended up in a car no better than mine, I'd be ahead of the game on two counts: I wouldn't be spending as much of my own money; and I'd have more time to devote to the business, which *needed* my attention at that point.

I found a ride for 1973 with Rolla Vollstedt, who had been around Indy car racing for years. He had some financial backing from the Norton Company, a major manufacturer of abrasives, which was just getting involved in racing but ended up sponsoring Indy cars well into the '80s. Norton's man at the track was a fellow named Bill

Hildick, who was a friend of Vollstedt's and has been a friend of mine ever since. The car was officially known as the Norton Spirit. It seemed like it was going to be a great program.

> **Bill Hildick, Norton Company motorsports represen-tative:** *In preparation for the 1973 season we took a show car to the company headquarters, in Worcester, Massachusetts, and to some of our plants. We had a lot of employees, 5,000 at the Worcester site alone, and we wanted them to see our car and our driver. Well, Bill was as good with those folks as anybody could possibly be. He got out there and drank coffee with the guys who made the grinding wheels, and they thought they'd died and gone to heaven. He became a real hero to everybody at the Norton Company, and my hero too.*

We went to the opening races, which gave us all a chance to get to know one another, and then it was time for Indianapolis. That was where things started to go wrong for us.

Rolla's car was essentially a copy of the previous year's McLaren. Guys used to do that all the time back then, just eyeball whatever design was the fastest and try to duplicate it. The Gurney Eagles got copied all the time; so did the McLarens. Of course the copies rarely went as fast as the genuine articles.

The big problem with Vollstedt's car at Indy was that it was absolutely unpredictable. I'd drive into a corner and feel just a hint of a push, which means that the front end just wants to plow straight on; then, halfway through the corner, the car would break loose—meaning that the rear tires would lose grip and the back end of the car would slide out—and I'd have to jump out of the throttle. That kind of situation will scare the hell out of any driver; normally you can deal with one specific handling characteristic, but you just cannot get comfortable in a car that constantly changes its behavior.

After a few days of this I'd had enough. I told Vollstedt that if we didn't sort out our chassis that car was going to bite me. Well, Rolla had a mechanic who just didn't like me, and this guy said, "Simpson, the problem is that you don't have the balls it takes to drive this place."

Whenever a team can't get up to speed, particularly at a big, fast track like Indianapolis, it is awfully easy to point fingers. A car has to be damn near perfect to be quick there, so drivers bitch a lot about handling. At the same time, not every driver has the fortitude to run that place wide open, so mechanics tend to blame the guy in the seat. This sort of thing happens all the time. But on this occasion I knew I was getting everything possible out of Rolla's car and I resented some helper saying that I wasn't.

I told him, "I'll tell you what, pal. Get on a bicycle and ride out to turn two. I'll drive this sucker through there without lifting and we'll see what happens."

On my next practice lap I went into turn two flat-out. The car had a tiny push, same as before, and then it got instantly loose at mid-corner, same as before. This time I never backed off; I just tried to wrestle it around. Well, I lost control. The car hit the outside wall first, then spun around and clobbered the inside wall on the backstretch, tearing down a hundred yards of debris fencing. It was a hell of a wreck. It knocked the engine out of the car and just about knocked my brains out, too. I mean, it rang my bell pretty good.

> **Bill Hildick:** *The morning after Bill's crash, I think every newspaper in the world had the same picture showing the Norton Spirit suspended on the back of a tow truck. I came into Gasoline Alley early that day, and the president of the Norton Company was on the telephone; he had called our garage. He said, 'Hildick, I've got to ask you something: is this a good thing or a bad thing?' He had been getting calls from all over the globe, telling him that our car was in the paper.*

I'll be honest: That crash frightened the shit out of me. But I proved my point, and later on USAC proved it again. See, when they impounded the car to do a post-crash inspection they found one of the axles had been installed incorrectly. As a result the suspension was binding up in the turns, which was the cause of our handling problem. Frankie Delroy, the USAC technical supervisor, was so upset about it that he confronted my mechanic—the same guy who had been so sure that I was the problem and that the car was fine—and ran his ass right out of Gasoline Alley.

They took stuff like that seriously at the Speedway, which was good because this was a very dangerous time to be a race driver. Speeds had shot up dramatically in the early '70s, thanks mostly to wings—just from 1971 to '72 the track record at Indy jumped from 179 miles per hour to more than 196!—and we were seeing some hellacious wrecks. In fact the day after my big crash, Art Pollard was killed.

Vollstedt had a back-up car, which we got out in time for the second weekend of qualifying, but our troubles hadn't ended. We blew an engine and to replace it we assembled a bunch of spare parts we had lying around. We didn't get it finished until early in the morning on Bump Day. Then we had all the usual problems you run into with these last-minute productions: loose oil lines, bad handling, stuff like that.

At Indy qualifying ends when the chief steward fires a starter's pistol at 5:00 P.M. on Bump Day. At 4:30 we took our final practice laps, and at last the car felt good. We were fast enough to make the race. We presented the car for the mandatory USAC pre-qualifying inspection, but rather than roll it right into the inspection station, Rolla chose to wait. Exactly why he waited I don't know, except that maybe he wanted to shave things pretty close to five o'clock so a faster car wouldn't bump us out once we'd gotten into the show. That's a common thing at the Speedway, to run the clock down. At any rate, there was a gap between our car and the inspection area, but both Rolla and I assumed that any other last-minute qualifiers would line up behind us.

That turned out to be a bad assumption. While Vollstedt and our guys were standing around, here came A.J. Foyt's crew, pushing a back-up car with George Snider in the seat. They snuck their car into that gap in front of us and the USAC guys started inspecting it. I was going crazy because there was very little time left; if you're not on the race track when the final gun fires, you're done. Sure enough, Snider's car passed inspection, he pulled away to start his qualifying run, and while he was out there the gun went off. I was left standing on pit road with a car that was plenty quick enough to get me into my first Indianapolis 500.

I was mad at the whole world. Mad at Vollstedt for putting us in that position, mad at Foyt's guys for cutting into the line, mad at USAC for allowing it to happen. Of course I shouldn't have expected any different from USAC; in those days A.J. could do no wrong as far as they were concerned. He was their hero. I complained to USAC that it was a bullshit call and then I told everybody who would listen that A.J. Foyt was nothing but a goddam cheater.

Foyt and I were still in our arch-enemy phase, so immediately everybody went running off to tell him what I had said. Pretty soon along came this fellow we used to call Big Pete. Big Pete used to work on Foyt's ranch, down in Texas; he was about six-and-a-half feet tall and four feet wide, with hands as big as footballs. Big Pete grabbed me, just reached straight out and lifted me a foot off the ground. He had incredible strength. Then he said, "You shouldn't talk about my boss that way."

*A.J. Foyt: What happened was pretty simple. Simpson got the shit slapped out of him.*

I tried to defend myself by taking a punch at Big Pete, but his arms were so long that I was just swinging away at thin air. The entire episode ended when Big Pete flipped me upside-down, walked me over to a trash can next to Dan Gurney's All American Racers garage, and stuffed me in headfirst.

*Wayne Leary, chief mechanic, All American Racers:*
*That whole thing happened right out in front of our garage. I*
*wasn't aware of what exactly had happened between them to*
*start it, but I figured it had to do with some smart-ass thing*
*Simpson had said about Foyt, and I was right. Anyway, it*
*didn't last very long; Big Pete was about three times the size*
*of Simpson, so there wasn't much of a fight. It was just,*
*bang, right into that 55-gallon can.*

It took me a while to crawl out of that can and a much longer time
to get over my anger at that whole situation. That incident typified
the way my racing life was going at the time. Everything was turning
out to be a struggle. I was constantly getting into hassles with USAC;
we had run-ins all the time. I fancied myself as the one guy who
wasn't going to put up with their guff, and that attitude certainly
didn't do me any good.

*Larry Burton: Simpson got in trouble with USAC every-*
*where we went. He was a wildman who didn't want to toe*
*the line, and they didn't like that. But I enjoyed being around*
*him because I didn't like to toe the line myself.*

*Steve Krisiloff, former Indy car driver: Simpson was*
*never too tolerant of somebody telling him he couldn't do a*
*certain thing. But that's like anybody who drives race cars,*
*I think. What I mean is, there are no followers driving race*
*cars. If you tell a race driver he can't do something, imme-*
*diately it gets the hair up on his back. And that's the way*
*Bill was.*

In hindsight I'd say that USAC and I were probably both to blame
for our problems. I had no real respect for authority, which was
wrong, but the USAC brass also took too dim a view of anyone they
thought was a nonconformist. The one exception was the late

Frankie Delroy; he was a wonderful man and the biggest supporter I ever had in USAC. Frankie was an old-line USAC guy, but he was open-minded enough to see that I was a devoted racer, not to mention a guy who was dedicating a lot of time and energy to making automobile racing safer.

Anyway, all these hassles started to bother me after that Indy and I sat out a pretty big chunk of the '73 season. Oh, I ran a little bit for Joe Hunt, a friend of mine from Torrance who was also the king of the racing magneto business, but his equipment wasn't a whole lot better than mine had been. The way things were looking, I was giving some serious thought to sitting out most of 1974 too. I did put together a deal to run the '74 Indy 500 for Dick Beith, but other than that I wasn't as excited about the sport as I once had been.

Then, in the spring of that year, a series of events turned my whole attitude around and made me feel racey again. That's just the way this sport is: A little taste of success can pump you up pretty quickly.

I went to Ontario in March for the California 500, even though I didn't have a ride. Honestly, I was just looking to hang out for a few days. But when I got there Frankie Delroy pointed out to me that John Martin had entered the race with his new McLaren—and that John had a back-up car I could probably get in.

> **John Martin:** *I had an old Brabham, a car which had originally belonged to Jack Brabham himself, and Bill dug up a little sponsorship from a place called Apple Annie's Speakeasy. And, well, we just kind of got together.*

To be honest, I wasn't too thrilled about John's car at first. That's not a knock against John—I had a lot of respect for his ability to prepare a race car—but his Brabham was built in 1968 and Indy cars went obsolete pretty quickly. This thing was practically an antique. On top of all that, John's only good engine was already in his McLaren. But I wanted to race, so John and I struck a deal: He'd furnish the car, I'd find an engine, and we'd split the prize money three ways: a third for him, a third for me and a third for whoever supplied the powerplant.

I went to A.J. Watson, who had gotten me through my Indianapolis rookie test back in '70, and told him I needed to borrow an engine. Watson talked to his boss, Bob Wilke, and an hour later I had myself a pretty strong Offy.

The California 500 was a week-long deal, so we hauled the car out to the track, stuck it in our assigned garage and worked on it day and night. It was me, Jerry Cook, Larry Burton and a few other guys. And there was this older guy who hung around and watched us work; he wore casual shirts and blue jeans with holes in them, and I figured he was just a race bum. Before you knew it, I had him running for hamburgers and polishing wheels and he was part of the team. Turns out he was Willett Brown, one of the richest men in Beverly Hills, who owned Hillcrest Cadillac and most of the choice real estate along Wilshire Boulevard. Willett enjoyed himself so much at Ontario that the next time I raced he sent a motorhome with two chefs and a waitress. No more burgers; we ate caviar and smoked salmon. He died a few years ago, but Willett's Hillcrest Collection still wins prizes at all of the big vintage car gatherings, and every time I hear that name I think about that week at Ontario.

When we finally got the car ready, there were maybe five minutes left in qualifying and I had yet to turn a single lap of practice. Dick King from USAC asked me if I needed an extra warm-up lap before my time-trial run; he thought we could use the extra shakedown time, I guess. I appreciated that, but it was too late to fix any problems we might have found in a shakedown run anyway.

I said, "Ain't nothing you can do for me. Just drop the green."

They did and off we went. I gritted my teeth, smoked it into turn one and the car stuck. And it stuck for the rest of that qualifying run. That little car drove like a dream. When we made the race everyone in the pits applauded because they'd gotten caught up in this Chinese fire drill we had put on all weekend.

That one qualifying run at Ontario showed me that I wanted to keep driving. I felt like a million bucks. I was smiling so much you'd have thought I had broken the track record at Indianapolis.

On race day, as soon as the green flag waved it was like everybody else was backing up. I was passing guys on the straightaways, passing them in the corners. Pretty soon this antique of ours was running in the top 10 and we were having the kind of day a team like ours wasn't supposed to have.

> **John Martin:** *That car was so little and light that it just flew down the straightaway. I mean, we had to run a gear two steps higher than anybody else's, just because it was so quick. In fact it was faster than my McLaren on the straight, but you had to really throw out the anchor when you got to the corner. Bill was having a pretty good run with that car.*

Then, slowly but surely, the handling went bad, which was a bigger problem than it is today because in 1974 we had no radio communication between driver and crew. There was no such thing as detailing a problem to your mechanic from behind the wheel and then having him adjust the car into tip-top shape. I fought that thing, and fought it some more, and it exhausted me. At halfway I was flat worn out; at the three-quarter point I was begging the car, "Please blow up. Let me out of here."

But the damned thing wouldn't blow up. So I just hung on. And we got a little lucky too, because some of the better cars ran into troubles of their own. At the end of the day we finished 14th, which was a better result, I'm sure, than any of us ever expected.

When it was over I just kind of sat back and said, "Wow." I was enthused about driving race cars again, which was a good thing because right around the corner was an event that ended up being the highlight of my racing life: the 1974 Indianapolis 500

# 5

# Racing with the Gods

I was on top of the world when Dick Beith signed me to drive his car, the American Kids Racer, at the Speedway in 1974. It was a nice car, a Gurney Eagle, but Beith was a strange guy, real stubborn about doing things his own way. That caused a few problems. For instance when I arrived in town, during the first week of May, the car was sitting on jackstands in our garage and I didn't see any wheels and tires anywhere. I asked Ted Swiontek, the chief mechanic, what the hell was going on. Turned out Beith didn't want to put any manufacturers' decals on his car, and that stopped us from getting a few things that were rather important—things like tires, fuel, oil, spark plugs. See, a lot of that stuff came free at Indianapolis as long as you ran the decal; but you couldn't *buy* it at any price.

I called Dick, out in California, and he just didn't seem to grasp any of this. He flew in the next day and proceeded to argue with everybody he could find. Now, I had done my share of arguing at the Speedway, but by '74 I had come to realize that it usually didn't get you anyplace. In the end, after we had wasted a couple of practice days, he gave in. The decals went on the car and we got the stuff we needed to put it on the race track.

We qualified on the first day. We were 20th, at just a tick over 181 miles per hour, even though the car had a little bit of a push. In fact on one occasion I got close enough to the wall to put some white paint on the right-side tires. Our speed should have had us in the race easily; normally 20th is plenty safe, since 33 cars get into the race, but then things got goofy.

On the second weekend of qualifying the temperature dropped dramatically. At Indianapolis cool means fast, because racing engines love cold air and the Speedway is a horsepower track. Suddenly even average cars were showing a lot of speed. That was bad news because once a car is bumped out of the field it's not allowed to re-qualify; the driver is allowed to try again in a back-up car, but we didn't have one.

As it turned out, we were OK. Some cars went faster than we did, but lots of others didn't and we were in the big show.

> **Ted Swiontek, Indy car mechanic:** *I had been going to Indy since 1964 and I'd been working on cars there since '65, so I had made the 500 a time or two. But, let me tell you, any time you make that race you're on top of the world.*

When the gun went off to signal the end of qualifying, a strange mix of feelings came over me. On one hand I was elated; I had earned a starting position at Indianapolis, which was obviously a career high. On the other hand I felt a good amount of trepidation. It was like, "Well, you're here. Now what?" I guess any driver who qualifies for his first 500 feels those same butterflies.

In the week leading up to the race Teddy and I went over how we were going to run it. The final practice on Thursday—Carburetion Day, they call it—went like a charm; we actually lapped faster than we had qualified, which was amazing because almost everybody else *lost* speed.

On the morning of the 500 I was as nervous as a whore in church, full of anxiety. Just walking out to that unique grid—at Indy, they line up the 33 starters in 11 rows of three—filled me with adrenaline. I got myself strapped in and when I heard Jim Nabors sing "Back Home Again in Indiana" it sent chills up my spine. It was absolutely the biggest thrill I have had in my entire life. If you're a race driver, that is *the* moment you live for.

We did our parade laps—in row seven I had Jerry Karl to my left in 19th, Pancho Carter to my right in 21st—and when we took the green flag I got on it. So did everybody else. When we got to the middle of the backstretch on the first lap, we were still three abreast. I discovered almost immediately that my car was just about perfect. I could put it anywhere I wanted to.

We gained a bunch of positions early on and I was feeling like it might be a pretty good day.

> ***Ted Swiontek:*** *Everything seemed to be going like clockwork. The car was fast and Bill was doing a good job. Early in the race he passed Lloyd Ruby, who had a very strong run—until running out of fuel in fourth place in the closing stages—and Bill pulled away from Ruby.*

Even as the race wore on and I settled into the kind of relaxed rhythm you need in a 500-miler, I still felt optimistic. Then, past the halfway point, I began to occasionally sense something wrong with the car; for some crazy reason the power would cut out for an instant. But it kept running and I kept chugging along. Then, at the three-quarter mark, the engine died in turn three.

I coasted into the pits and I saw Ted shaking his head, clearly upset. He had a wrench in his hand, which told me that he had a pretty good idea what the problem was.

> ***Ted Swiontek:*** *You're always anticipating trouble, but you can't anticipate everything. The very last thing I had done on Saturday was change the fuel filter on the car, just as a precaution. But here we were, in the race and the engine was not getting any fuel. It would idle OK, but as soon as you blipped the throttle it would die. It was obvious that there was something wrong in the fuel system, probably a blockage in the filter.*

As soon I saw Teddy start unbolting the fuel lines, I had a pretty good idea too what the problem was.

I had learned, every May since 1970, that Indianapolis is not a good place to cut corners. At the Speedway you could nickel-and-dime yourself right out of the picture. Well, Dick Beith learned that the hard way in '74. He had rented an old refueling rig from somebody, even though you could buy a brand-new stainless-steel rig for a little over $1,000. I had told Beith I didn't feel good about that old tank; those things tended to suffer from corrosion if they weren't maintained properly. I even offered to buy a new one myself, which made Beith sort of snippy. He told me to pay attention to driving the car and let him worry about running the operation. He had the crew take the side cover off the rented fueling rig and then he had his son crawl in to swab it out.

Now, as I watched Ted Swiontek unbolt the fuel lines on my car, and as Teddy and I both watched the rust pour out, it was clear what had happened: The refueling tank had not been sufficiently cleaned; from our very first pit stop we had been taking on contaminated fuel. Eventually the rust packed the car's fuel filter solid and the engine died.

> **Ted Swiontek:** *We had to change the fuel filter on pit road, which cost us a lot of time. That's what I mean about how you can't anticipate everything; we had just changed that filter the night before the race and figured we wouldn't be needing another one, so we didn't have a spare in the pits. While I was taking the bad filter out, one of our crewmen ran back to the garage—which was pretty near a half-mile away—to grab a new one. With the race day crowd, it probably took him 10 minutes to get there and back.*

Teddy got the car's fuel system cleaned out and we got back into the race. Unfortunately, because you're only allowed to take on fuel from your own supply, the problem was bound to recur. It did, and

Teddy fixed it again. Each time we returned to the race track with a fast car, but all our speed meant nothing. We were hopelessly out of contention. Worst of all, we had beaten ourselves.

Finally, with just a couple of laps to go, we burned a piston, which is what typically happens when an engine is starved for fuel. Because there had been a pretty high rate of attrition in the 500, our official finish wasn't all that bad; we were placed 13th.

When I climbed out of the car I could hear the crowd in the paddock seats applauding. They obviously appreciated the effort we had put in all day long. Their support was nice, but I was never more dejected in my life than I was at that moment. All I could think about was what might have been. When our car had been running properly I was ahead of Bill Vukovich Jr., and Billy ended up finishing third! Even after the engine started cutting out, we were on a pace to finish in the top 10. There was no way I was going to be happy with 13th.

It started raining shortly after the finish, but I just sat there on the pit wall, in the rain, pissed off. Ted Swiontek was feeling the same way. By the time I got back to our garage his toolbox was sitting outside. He said, "I ain't working like this no more." And he quit.

> **Ted Swiontek:** *I was pretty unhappy. I got my toolbox out in Gasoline Alley and loaded it right into my truck. See, that was one of the first times I felt I was involved with a competitive car at Indianapolis, so I was very disappointed.*

It was a classic case of how Indy can strain a guy emotionally. I felt it too.

The race right after the 500 was at Milwaukee, and we were actually pretty stout there—we started last because we had trouble in qualifying, and charged up to finish eighth—but it didn't come close to erasing those bitter Indianapolis memories. After just two more starts I climbed out of the American Kids Racer.

I was right back where I'd been a year earlier: disillusioned and standing on the sidelines. Over the last half of 1974 and all of '75 I ran just one Indy car race, the '74 finale at Phoenix with Rolla Vollstedt. We finished 11th.

I spent most of my time at my factory, trying to keep a handle on business because the company was still on the rise. I didn't even bring a car to Indianapolis in 1975, although I ended up driving something anyway. My friend Steve Krisiloff broke his leg in a crash on the first day of practice and his mechanic, Don Koda, asked me to get in Stevie's car in case he didn't heal in time. I ran a bunch of laps and we were fast enough to qualify, but Krisiloff was ready by the time Pole Day came around. It was his ride, so I couldn't feel bad about getting out. I had a few offers to jump into other cars before qualifying, but none of them really appealed to me.

Like I said: I was disillusioned. I had been running Indy cars since 1968 and I was still having more bad days than good ones. But every so often I'd sneak back and run a road race someplace—the SCCA's Formula 5000 class had a hot little series—and do well enough to convince myself that I belonged in a race car.

I decided to take one more serious crack at USAC with my own team. Driving for other people had been a relief, sure, but the results weren't much better than when I ran on my own. Plus, thanks to the growth of the business, I had a few more dollars to play with this time around. I bought myself a year-old Gurney Eagle and hired Ted Swiontek to work on it. I thought we had bonded really well when I drove for Dick Beith.

Together we went back to the Speedway in May of 1976 determined to do better than we'd done in '74.

Ah, the best-laid plans. . . .

As it turned out, '76 ended up being another one of those weird Indy years, weather-wise. It was hotter than hell when we qualified on the first Saturday, but we had what seemed to be a really safe speed. In fact I felt so confident that I jumped a flight back to Los Angeles and I didn't plan on coming back until it was time for the Carburetion Day practice. I was sitting on that airliner, telling myself, "Man, we're stylin'. We're in the 500 again."

Well, we weren't. Ted called me during the week. He said, "Hey, the temperature here has dropped about 20 degrees."

Again: Cool means fast. I was back at the Speedway in time for the second weekend of qualifying. I jumped in the car for the morning practice and instantly hot-lapped several miles per hour faster than I had qualified. I knew right away that we were in trouble; if we could gain that much speed, so could everyone else.

> **Ted Swiontek:** *At Indianapolis, when the weather's with you you're in good shape; when it's against you, well, you're in trouble. That same year Mario Andretti missed the first weekend of qualifying because he was off racing Formula One, so he qualified on the second weekend. And Mario had the fastest qualifying speed in the field. He didn't get to start on the pole because he wasn't a first-day qualifier, but he had the fastest speed.*

Long before qualifying ended I told Ted, "We may as well start getting this thing set up for Milwaukee. We're about to get bumped out of the Indy 500." And that's exactly what happened. We missed the race by two spots. May of 1976 felt an awful lot like every May had from 1970 through '73.

We ran that Eagle several more times, and it was a solid race car. We finished eighth at Milwaukee and Michigan, and we could always qualify in the middle of the pack. But it wasn't a car that was ever going to put you at the front of the pack, which was where I wanted to be.

The best chassis at the time was the McLaren, and the best team was Roger Penske's. By this point Roger and I had forgotten our old differences and become almost friendly, so I approached him about buying one of his McLarens. The California 500 was coming up; I had always liked Ontario and I had been quick there even in sub-par equipment. I wanted to see what I could do in a top-shelf car.

I guess Roger wanted to see too. He said, "Simpson, I'll sell you this car, but only if you promise to race it exactly the way we hand it over. You can't change a thing."

I agreed to that because Roger always had a bunch of smart people working for him. I had some great help too—Jerry Cook and Steve Robey, just to name two—but Penske's guys were plugged into the latest McLaren technology. We went to Ontario and Roger's boys delivered the car right to the track. I mean, they rolled that McLaren straight into my garage and told me it was ready to run. And, boy, was it ever.

When they opened the track I ran two warm-up laps and then I gassed it up a bit. On my third time past the pits my guys hung out a board showing me my speed. It was a lot faster than I had ever gone at Ontario and I hadn't even settled into a comfortable rhythm, so I figured they were just jacking around with me. Well, the next time by they showed me an even higher speed, and the lap after that, higher still.

I pulled into the pits and said, "Look, guys, quit screwing around."

They said, "Bill, that's how fast you're running."

They weren't kidding. I went out and ran some more laps, just to see how the car handled on different parts of the track, and whether I ran high or low the speed was there. I said, "Let's park this thing. We don't need to run it anymore."

Come qualifying day, we ended up 14th on the grid without even trying hard, and I was shaking my head. All I kept thinking was, "Man, this is almost too easy."

When they dropped the green flag for the California 500, I hauled ass. I mean, I could run with anybody. I passed Al Unser like he was tied to a tree and the next thing I knew I was battling with Al's brother Bobby. Pretty soon I was leading the race.

Just a few months earlier I had missed the show at Indy and now I was holding my own at Ontario with some of the toughest guys ever to strap into Indy cars. When things go right, racing can be a real blast.

Late in the race we were still running well and then suddenly the engine began losing power. My heart sank. By now despair was a feeling I knew all too well.

What happened at Ontario was a lot like what happened at Indy in '74: We got beat by a problem we should never have allowed to happen. I had noticed after qualifying that the inlet hose on the turbocharger was showing some age, but I guess I figured that if it was good enough for Roger Penske it was good enough for Bill Simpson. In the race the hose split, which robbed the engine of every last bit of turbo boost. No boost, no horsepower.

Robey and Cook and the guys got it fixed, but we lost about 15 laps. We were still really fast—in fact I passed every car on the track once I re-entered the race—but we were hopelessly out of contention. We ended up finishing right where we started, in 14th.

That 1976 California 500 may have been my best Indy car race, in terms of how competitive we were and how well I drove. Yet at the time I had a hard time seeing it as a great day. I left Ontario feeling dejected. I had gotten a brief taste of what it was like to race at the highest level, and loved it, but I knew in my heart that we would never be able to sustain that kind of an effort. Come the next race, Penske wasn't going to be there guiding us along, and teams like his were probably going to pull away from us again.

I was right. That McLaren never again ran as well as it did at Ontario. I took it to Indy in '77 with Dean Williams as my chief mechanic, Gary Rovazzini as his assistant, and help from Jerry Cook and Don Koda. We struggled to find speed and it frustrated the hell out of me. I woke up every morning hoping that when I pulled back the motel-room curtains I'd see rain. And I was telling myself the whole time, "You're at Indianapolis, where you've always wanted to be . . . yet you don't really want to be here. This is not the way a race driver should feel."

Where I wanted to be—or, more correctly, where I knew I ought to be—was back in Torrance, taking care of business. The company was at a point where it was demanding more and more attention, and I found myself giving it that attention even when it should have been the farthest thing from my mind.

> **Gary Rovazzini:** *During practice Bill would come in and tell us what the car was doing, and while we were making the necessary changes he'd be on the telephone, checking in with the factory in California. Then he'd get back in the car and run some more.*

I kept going out every day, practicing, trying to get faster, because that was all I knew how to do. Then one morning, as I came out of turn two and headed down the backstretch, I caught myself glancing at the front suspension and thinking, "What would happen if that wishbone broke? What would happen if that wheel came off? If I crash and get hurt, who's going to run the company while I heal?"

The last thing a race driver should be doing at 200 miles per hour is letting his mind wander. I pulled in, thinking I just needed a few minutes to regain my focus. Dean asked me what was wrong and I said, "Nothing. I just want to think a few things out."

I sat there while the crew checked the car and I said, "OK, let's go." I ran a few more laps and we were quick; quick enough to qualify, no question. And then, coming off turn two again, my attention started to drift once more. I caught myself thinking about a phone call I was supposed to make and about some material I needed to purchase. By the time I got those thoughts sorted out, I was just about at the turn-in point for turn three.

What I thought at the time was pretty raw: "Fuck this."

I pulled back into the pits and told Dean and the guys to take the car back to the garage. Then I sat on the pit wall. Every so often someone would wander over to chat, the way people always do, and I'd ask them to leave me alone. It was decision-making time and I knew it. I was looking at the end of my driving career.

I sat there for maybe 30 minutes and in that time I realized two things: that this had been more than just a brief lapse in focus; and that I was a good candidate for busting not only my own ass, but somebody else's too. I walked back to Gasoline Alley, head down, still not entirely sure what I was going through. But as soon as I reached my garage and opened the door, I knew one thing: I was now an ex-race driver.

Dean and Gary asked me what was wrong. I shut the garage door, pointed at the car and said, "You will never see me sit in one of these things again."

> **Gary Rovazzini:** *Bill was very honest. He said, 'I'm thinking about business when I should be trying to drive a race car. This is crazy.' And he told us he was quitting.*

I told those guys that my head just wasn't in it anymore. They accepted that. Both Gary and Dean had been around long enough to know that driving at Indianapolis isn't something you can do halfway.

I stuck to my vow: Never again did I sit in an Indy car. Of course I'd be lying if I said that retirement was easy. I missed the hell out of driving race cars; hell, I *still* miss it. But, in all honesty, I had no regrets. I felt like I took whatever talent I had as far as I could possibly have taken it.

> **Wayne Leary:** *Simpson wasn't a bad driver. He wasn't a threat to us when we had Bobby [Unser] in Gurney's car; our competition came from Rutherford, Foyt and Johncock, people like that. But Simpson had some pretty good days. If we were the upper class, he was kinda like upper-middle-class.*

> **Johnny Rutherford:** *Bill had some ability as a driver, but he just didn't stick around very long.*

> **Gary Rovazzini:** *He had some good runs. When he ran*

*Indy for Dick Beith, he did a very good job. And when I had*
*worked with him earlier, in the early '70s, we had some real*
*good races. Bill was a good race car driver.*

   ***Tom Smith:*** *If he'd had a few bucks behind him early on,*
*and been able to concentrate on racing rather than building*
*a business, Bill could have developed into one of the top*
*drivers. I really believe that.*

I've said this before and I'll say it again: I wasn't a Foyt, or an Andretti, or an Unser, or a Rutherford. On my best days I could sometimes run with them, but on *their* best days they were in another
league. Those guys were the sport's lead actors and the rest of us
were their supporting cast.

I'll show you what I mean: We were at Trenton in '76, running
one of the few races that was covered on TV back then. I think it was
on ABC's "Wide World of Sports." It was colder than a well-digger's
ass and the cars weren't sticking worth a damn because it was tough
to keep the tires at optimum temperature. I was running in the middle of the pack with a few laps to go when the rear suspension broke
on my Eagle. It was no big deal; all I had to do was putt around and
I could limp to the finish. I pulled out of the groove and slowed
down. On the backstretch I saw Foyt coming fast in my mirrors. That
wasn't surprising, because he had been leading, but I noticed white
streaks around his front tires. Those streaks, I knew, were the blur of
the stickers that are on every new tire. It turned out that Foyt had
gotten a flat and pitted and had just come back onto the track.

When he passed me, he was flying. I thought about his speed, his
new tires and the cold temperature, and I said to myself, "There is
no way he is going to make it through turn three."

And he didn't. He drove straight into the wall.

There was a yellow flag to clean up his debris, and when we
cruised back around Foyt was standing on the track, shaking his fist
at me like his wreck had been *my* fault. I couldn't figure out what

that was all about. Later somebody told me A.J. had complained on television that I had put him into the fence.

> ***Robin Miller, motorsports columnist,*** **Indianapolis Star:** *Foyt screwed up and crashed, and he had to blame someone, so he got on national TV and blamed Simpson. Hell, Simpson was far enough away from him that he may as well have been on the other side of the track, but Foyt badmouthed the shit out of him.*

That night I bumped into A.J. at the hotel and I asked him about it. He looked right at me and said, "Hey, this was a TV race. I had to blame somebody." I had to admit that made sense. As a member of the supporting cast, I was the perfect foil.

> ***Robin Miller:*** *If you were a major star back then—Foyt, Rutherford, Bobby Unser, Mario—you had to have a good excuse. And Simpson was a good guy for Foyt to blame.*

Foyt and I kind of bickered back and forth for years. We're friends today, but we weren't in my driving days. Still, I know now—and I'm sure I knew then—what an honor it was just to be on the same track with him. The same went for Mario, Bobby and Al, and the other giants of that period.

To me those guys were the racing equivalent of Greek gods. I got to be out there with them and that's important to me. Any driver in the world would be proud to have raced when I raced, where I raced and against the people I raced with.

And I can't imagine that anything in the world compares to starting the Indianapolis 500 alongside guys like them. Indy will always be special to me. It broke my heart a few times, just like it broke a lot of hearts. But it also gave me the greatest high of my life.

That thing I said a minute ago, about racing with the gods? Well, Indianapolis was the place where I raced them on their turf.

# 6

# Down to Business

I climbed out of race cars thinking my decision was best for the business, and time has proven me right on that. But I was very wrong on one other point: I had initially believed that throwing myself headlong into the day-to-day operation of the company might replace the thrill I got from racing. It didn't even come close.

Don't get me wrong: There is a real buzz involved in closing a profitable deal and I get a lot of excitement out of, say, watching a new Simpson product catch on with the public. But once you've driven race cars, driven them all the way from nowhere to Indianapolis, nothing else compares.

I liked the fact that all my efforts were now being focused in the same direction. I liked the fact that I no longer had to constantly swap my priorities back and forth, from the office to the race car. I liked the fact that the load on my shoulders had been lightened. I was in most respects a pretty happy guy. But I was a pretty happy guy with a big, big void in his life.

Think about it: To me driving race cars was the ultimate high and I had been able to reach for that high for roughly 20 years. Now that high was gone. I have to be honest—it took me three or four years for me to really get used to that.

Maybe that's why I didn't get *totally* away from the competitive side of the sport; I stayed involved for several years as a car owner. I wasn't sure I'd be happy watching my cars rather than driving them myself, but something that happened in the 1976 California

500—the race in which I'd run so well in that ex-Penske McLaren—
had told me I might find it satisfying.

For a while I had been close to a young Baja racer by the name
of Rick Mears. He was a nice kid from a racing family known as the
Mears Gang and, in 1975, after he had started dabbling in road racing with the SCCA, I gave him a test at Willow Springs. I had a Formula 5000 car built in Argentina by Oresta Berta, who was using
our team to help him develop the design a little bit. The car was not
really a competitive piece, but we took it out to Willow and let Rick
get some laps in it. I saw something in Rick at that test, and I had
a feeling that before long a lot more people would see something in
Rick too.

### Rick Mears, four-time Indianapolis 500 winner:

*I was going quicker and quicker and quicker every lap, and I
guess Bill told one of his guys, 'You watch, he's going to go
off the track in turn nine before too long.' See, turn nine at
Willow Springs is a fast corner, but it has kind of a tricky
little blind exit. And, sure enough, I dropped a wheel off into
the dirt. But I just ran along there in the dirt for a bit, gath-
ered it up, got it back on the track and kept going. Hell, I was
used to running off-road, so driving off the edge of the track
was no big deal. Simpson laughed about that.*

Rick and I hit it off really well. I had pretty much resigned myself
to the fact that business was going to keep me out of a race car for
most of 1975, so I had this idea: Why not put Rick in the F5000 car?
And maybe, if things worked out, in the Indy car sometime down the
road? So Rick and I signed a deal. I found out later that it was the
first contract he'd ever had.

He did some F5000 races for me and you could see him getting
better each time out. By the middle of the '76 season he was more
than ready for an Indy car and I was thinking about starting him
off at Ontario. But there was a problem. As soon as I bought that

McLaren from Roger Penske, along came a fellow named Art Sugai looking to buy my old Eagle, which I had planned on running for Rick. Fortunately, the problem solved itself. Art had a few drivers in mind but he hadn't hired anybody, so I told him I wouldn't sell him the Eagle unless he stuck Rick in the seat for the California 500. Sugai went along with that and Rick had himself a ride.

Some of the top USAC officials weren't too thrilled with the idea of this off-road kid running in a 500-mile Indy car race, which shows you all you need to know about their ability to spot talent. I actually had to post sort of a bond—I used my house for collateral—as a form of insurance in case Rick ran into somebody.

I raced the McLaren and Rick ran my number 38 Eagle, the same car I had been driving when I got bumped at Indianapolis that May. Nothing Rick had ever driven could compare, speed-wise, to an Indy car at a place like Ontario, but he looked right at home from the moment the track opened. He qualified pretty easily, starting 20th.

I remember telling Rick prior to the race, "Just run this thing conservatively, stay out of trouble, and you'll be OK."

Well, Rick was better than OK. He was fast—and smooth and smart. Oh, he didn't exactly run up front, but you have to keep in mind that he was driving a car whose best days had come and gone. Take it from me: Mears was terrific that Sunday at Ontario.

> **Rick Mears:** *I knew there was no way I was going to out-run the fast guys with that car, so my game plan was to out-live 'em, if I could. I just did my best to keep my nose clean. I mean, I ran hard, but at the same time I made sure I didn't make any mistakes.*

I got to see Rick in action a lot that day because in the McLaren I was fast enough to lap him a few times, and there's one memory that has stuck with me: Every time I came up behind him, I'd see Rick's eyes in the mirror. He'd notice me and he'd move over real quick to get out of the boss's way. I mean, he'd just jerk that thing to the left. He was only trying to be helpful, but he was making me a nervous wreck. I kept thinking, Don't throw the car around like that, Rick—you'll crash, and I'll have to sit here and watch it!

When I lost all that time in the pits with the broken turbo hose, Rick made up the ground I'd gained on him and then some. In the end he finished eighth to my 14th. That meant I had to endure a lot of ribbing from him after the race, which pissed me off to the point where I had to find some way to get even.

Earlier in the week I had seen this guy in the pits airbrushing T-shirts. I found him and said, "See that 38 car sitting over there? I want you to airbrush that car on a shirt, right now. And underneath that I want you to put these words: 'Mears Gang Sucks.'"

I put that shirt on and walked back into Rick's garage. He got a kick out of that. The only problem was, a bunch of his family and friends had arrived and most of them had no idea who I was. They figured I was just some loudmouth looking for trouble. I'm telling you, we almost had us a brawl before Rick calmed them all down.

After that weekend the car belonged to Art Sugai and Mears ran it a few more times. He finished ninth at both Texas and Phoenix and USAC named him its 1976 Indy car Rookie of the Year.

Everybody knows what became of Rick from there. He turned all the right heads in a hurry and ended up spending the rest of his Indy car career driving for Roger Penske. By the time he retired, after the 1992 season, Mears had won just about everything, including four Indianapolis 500s and three CART titles. To this day I take a lot of pride in whatever role I played in helping him along.

> **Roger Penske:** *Bill had a lot to do with Rick's career. Rick drove Bill's Indy car, and it was later on that I picked up on Rick's ability. I guess I've got to thank Bill for getting Rick Mears started, because he sure turned over a great driver.*

I'd like to say my race teams went on to fare as well as Rick did, but that would be a lie. I fielded Indy cars for Dennis Firestone as well as Super Vee and American Racing Series cars for Pete Halsmer, Tom Hessert, Juan Fangio II, Scott Acheson, Kenny Johnson, Tero Palmroth, Bobby Unser Jr. and a few other guys, including my sons, Dave and Jeff. Later on I ran a NASCAR Busch Series stock car team for Dave, but we didn't have much success there.

I liked campaigning my own cars because it kept me as close to the action as a non-driver could be. In fact I enjoyed running my fleet of Super Vees—at one time I had five—as much as anything I'd ever done; that series was fairly affordable, low-key and yet very intense. You'd have 35 or 40 cars show up and their lap times would be incredibly close. But there's no question that once I got out of the driver's seat, owning race cars just wasn't as appealing as it had been.

And that was probably a good thing because the challenge of running the company full-time was turning out to be greater than I had counted on. For me, steering a business was tougher than steering a race car. I mean, anybody can run a business; all it takes is money. It's running one correctly, and making it grow, that's difficult. You've got to be on your toes at all times, looking out for things that can go wrong while at the same time looking out for opportunities to do better. In my case the process became all-consuming.

It was kind of funny, really. The business had been the biggest constant in my life since 1958 and I often called it my baby, but only in the late '70s did I become its full-time parent. Since that time it really has been a parental relationship. I have nurtured it and fed it like a child; it has given me some problems, like a child; it has changed over time and is still changing, like a child.

We were a healthy company at the point when I quit racing. In fact I had moved a portion of the operation into a new industrial park I started in Torrance, called Gasoline Alley West, where we played landlord to a number of speed-equipment manufacturers and racers. Still, I knew we weren't operating at anything close to our potential. I hadn't paid enough attention to marketing or to what our competition was doing. I told myself I was paying attention, but the truth is, while I was racing *and* running the business, I simply didn't have the desire to take on any more responsibility than I already had.

Over a period of a few years I realized how badly I had neglected the company by not going after what could have been ours. I tried to turn all that around fast, probably too fast. In a period that lasted from 1978 to '80 I devoted more physical and mental energy to working than I had in years. What I did, really, was attack the business the way I had once attacked racing.

I never had any kind of a concrete goal for the company, never had a time-line for reaching any specific objectives. All I wanted was for it to keep growing. I spent my weekdays digging into new ideas and new manufacturing techniques, and on weekends I talked to as many people as I could at various race tracks. I'll bet I averaged 50 races a year in the late '70s and early '80s, races of all kinds. The way I looked at it, that was the best kind of field research I could do.

It was a critical point in the company's life, and it was all in my hands. For a guy who hadn't had any formal business training, I think I did all right. I'm not sure many other eighth-grade dropouts could have done as well.

In the late 1960s there was a point when my lack of education had scared me; there were things about business and commerce that I just didn't understand. I solved that problem the only way I knew how: I found the books I needed to teach myself what I figured I should know. Ten years later I was awfully glad I had done that.

Still, I'm sure my leadership methods were anything but conventional. For example, I never looked at the bottom line as being the most important thing for the company. That's probably a strange philosophy for the guy whose name is on the building, but I figured it was better to stick to the game plan I had back in 1958: to do whatever I could to take the danger out of my chosen sport. That boiled down to putting the racer first.

I'll concede that in the beginning some of that was selfishness. The life I saved may have been my own. But even later I believed that our ultimate priority should be building and selling the finest equipment, regardless of how that impacted our profit margin.

> **Dick Berggren, editor,** Speedway Illustrated *magazine: In the winter of 1977–'78 I went to see Simpson in Torrance. I was interested in showing him that I cared about safety and that he ought to advertise his stuff in* Stock Car Racing *magazine, of which I was then editor. Well, Bill changed the focus of our meeting entirely. He took me through his shop and showed me some things that were completely unknown to racers across America.*
>
> *At that time everybody figured the only thing you needed to wear was a Nomex fire suit. But what Bill showed me— and he was very smart to show me rather than to tell me, because if he had just told me I might have taken it as a sales pitch—was a little test he had. He took a piece of the old- style monofilament Nomex, the stuff everybody was wearing at the time, and put it in some kind of a holder. Then he lit a Bunsen burner and directed the flame toward that piece of cloth. Behind this piece of cloth Simpson had rigged up a thermometer. I had never seen this done before. What he showed me was that in a matter of seconds the heat trans- ferred from one side of that Nomex to the other. I mean, you could watch that thermometer just go crazy. Simpson said, "Do you know what this means? This means that if a guy is wearing just a single-layer fire suit he's got only these few seconds before he is critically burned."*
>
> *Then he took a piece of a new fabric called Nomex III and did a comparison burn test between that material and the monofilament Nomex. The monofilament quickly hardened and had holes burned in it; the Nomex III held its shape much better. It was clearly a superior fabric.*
>
> *The combined impact of those two tests led to a story in*

*the magazine, a story that transformed the way a lot of racers thought about fire protection. And it transformed the way I thought about Simpson. He hadn't shown me these things just to sell product; in fact what he did was going to hurt him, short-term, because he had so much of this old mono-filament Nomex lying around. But he didn't care about that. What he cared about were the racers.*

*I'll give you another example of that. For a long time, most drivers raced in sneakers—old rubber-and-canvas sneakers. When I was driving a sprint car, that's what I always wore. They were well ventilated, they were comfortable and they gave you a good feel for the pedals. So when Simpson showed me a new fireproof shoe he was making, I said, "You're going to lose your shirt on those. You won't sell enough of those things to make a buck." He looked at me and said, "Berggren, I don't give a shit." Then he explained to me how, in a fire, sneakers would melt right to your feet. I went home and put a pair of my own sneakers on the feet of a mannequin we used as a model and lit 'em on fire with a little bit of gasoline. Well, those sneakers melted to the mannequin's feet, just like Simpson said they would. I never wore sneakers again when I raced.*

**Bobby Allison:** *For the longest time I raced in Hush Puppies, the same casual shoes I wore to kick around in, and I used to blister my feet all the time. I just accepted that as one of the discomforts you had to endure if you wanted to race. There were even a few times when I was proud of the fact that I kept going despite the pain of my blistered feet, when other people might have pulled out of the race. But as Simpson got further and further into the kind of technology that could protect you from the heat that caused those blisters, that was the end of those Hush Puppies.*

I guess I looked at it this way: If we kept putting the racer first, we would make the best products. And from there it would follow that the bottom line would be positively impacted.

I did something else too that might have been unusual for a guy leading a company of our size: I refused to do anything by committee. I never saw any need to hold meetings when I could make a decision myself. Early on I learned that everybody has an opinion on everything—I mean, if we all liked white, we wouldn't need paint stores—but as long as it said "Simpson" on the door I was better off making the big decisions myself. That way if we made a mistake, it was *my* mistake. I'd be sure to get input from people I respected, and I would carefully digest what they said, but in the end I always made the final decision based on my gut instinct.

Whether that theory is right or wrong in every application is not for me to say. But I do know that in our specific case it must have worked because the company started growing like a weed in 1978. And, despite a bunch of ups and downs we've faced since that time, we've never really looked back.

I had some outside help too, from a lot of folks. One of my biggest influences in those days was a fellow by the name of Tom Sheddon, who was kind of my mentor. Tom, who is retired now, used to be the president of Cragar Industries. Whenever I had a problem I'd jump in my car, head over to his office in Compton, and sit with Tom a while. He was a guy who was very successful in this business and I just looked up to him a whole lot.

What also helped me was plenty of luck, in that my timing could not have been better. Prior to the late '70s nobody referred to what we did in motorsports as an "industry." There were race tracks, there were racers and there were companies supplying products and services, but no one was presumptuous enough to think of this as an industry. Then, as the decade came to a close, we all began to take a long look at the enormous amounts of money swirling around: money being poured *into* racing, money being generated *by* racing. That was when our sport began to take itself seriously, and the outside world began to take it seriously too. Motor racing was home to several multi-million-dollar companies and it was silly to think of it as anything *less* than a legitimate industry.

So, as the 1970s melted into the '80s, the motorsports industry began to ride a wave of success. Trade shows, which had been a rarity, began to sprout and grow, and different organizations began to have a strong voice in representing the various constituencies that all came under racing's umbrella. One such organization was SEMA, which had already been around a while. In fact SEMA— which originally stood for the Speed Equipment Manufacturers Association but is now the Specialty Equipment Marketing Association—was launched when 67 of us met in the '60s to discuss the idea of having a unified voice in our dealings with the powers that ran racing.

The bottom line was that a lot of us felt like we had been getting kicked around. I'll give you a first-hand example: In the early '60s, in addition to hauling my dragster to NHRA events all over the country, I would bring along a pickup truck with a sewing machine in the back. That way if a fellow had a problem with a parachute at the track, I would jump right in and sew it up for him, free. Well, somebody at the National Hot Rod Association decided I ought to be paying a fee for the privilege of doing business in the pit area. My argument was that since I wasn't charging anybody a dime, I wasn't doing business—I was providing a service.

Other manufacturers were having similar problems. SEMA was one of the groups that helped solve those problems. It was a very early step in the process of the tracks, the racers and the suppliers realizing that we were all a part of something that was bigger than any of us.

By the late '70s that step had become a march. Racing's fan base grew, advertising opportunities knocked, and the wave just got bigger. Simpson Race Products was right there, riding that wave. In some respects I really feel like we were among the leaders pushing that wave.

> **Dick Berggren:** *There is no question but that Bill Simpson was one of the pioneers of the so-called motorsports industry. I mean, if you see the potential in something before everyone else does, you're a pioneer. And he was one of the first people to see that there was a huge market out there for racing and racing-related items.*

We were among the earliest companies to see the wisdom in what today's marketing types call "developing a brand." What that means, in basic terms, is that instead of just marketing our safety products to a customer base limited to racers, we put the Simpson logo on a wide range of items, including apparel. This was kind of a legacy of my straight-line days; around the drag strips there had always been T-shirts with product logos on them. Ed Iskenderian and Howard Johansson, who were rivals in the cam business, started all that. If you wanted to be cool in the early '60s you wore either an "Isky Cams" shirt or a "Howard's Cams" shirt. Well, we did the same thing in the '70s, but with all kinds of clothing.

Our first real hit was an item that is now universally referred to as "the Simpson jacket." It was a black quilted jacket with three stripes—red, orange, yellow—on each sleeve. I'll tell you when I first realized how popular that jacket was. I was in Indianapolis and I went out to the State Fairgrounds with some friends to watch the Hulman Hundred USAC dirt car race. We sat in the grandstands and on this crisp autumn day you could see hundreds of those jackets floating around in the infield pit area. This drunk guy sitting behind us said, "Man, I don't know which driver all those people in the black jackets are with, but whoever he is, he's sure got one hell of a pit crew."

I thought about that for a long time and what it showed me was this: While there may have been thousands of *racers*, there were *millions* of race *fans*. And that number was growing daily because auto racing was really spreading in popularity. Any firm interested in growing with the sport, I figured, needed to look beyond pit road.

That notion evolved into what today is a line of clothing for racers and fans alike—Simpson T-shirts, sweatshirts, hats, you name it.

It was also during this period that I started getting involved personally in more types of racing. Through my driving career I knew everyone in the Indy car pit area and I still had plenty of drag-racing friends, but there were other segments of the sport I had all but ignored. I set out to change that. As usual, I went at it full-tilt.

I followed my old friend Mario Andretti for a whole Formula One season, attending all the Grand Prix races, and that paid off. There was a period, before the really big money came in and the European safety companies started offering ridiculous endorsement deals to the top drivers, when almost every F1 racer ran Simpson products. And I started dabbling more in NASCAR at a time when Winston Cup racing was really starting to take off. But I didn't just focus on the so-called big leagues. I also went to sprint car races, midget races and short-track stock car races all over the country.

Looking back, that was really an interesting period. One week I'd be flying to London on the Concorde and the next week I'd be anywhere from a drag strip to a half-mile dirt oval, meeting racers at every stop. It was great for the company because it put me in touch with people I had rarely spoken to by phone, let alone spent five minutes with. I'd be at a sprint car race and I'd say to a driver, "I see you wear Simpson gear. Well, *I'm* Simpson. Is there anything I can help you with? Anything you want to complain about?"

This gave us a lot of credibility with the average racer, particularly the grassroots short-track guys. They seemed to think it was kind of cool that Simpson was not just a label on a fire suit, that there was an actual person running the company and here he was, at their home track, asking for their input.

That doesn't happen with every manufacturer they deal with. I mean, if you're a sprint car racer who has been a lifelong Goodyear customer, Mr. Goodyear isn't going to walk through the mud at some little dirt track looking for your opinion, because there *ain't* a Mr. Goodyear. In our case, even if they knew a guy named Bill Simpson existed, they hadn't had contact with him. But they damn sure did now.

> ***Rusty Wallace, 1989 NASCAR Winston Cup champion:*** *It's his name on the product: Simpson. It's not, you know, the Acme Firesuit Company. It's Bill Simpson's company and that's who you deal with. If you have a problem with anything that's got Simpson's name on it, all you need to do is call Simpson himself and the problem is over.*

It was an ideal way to grow the company, and for a long time that was how I justified all this traveling around. Today I'm able to see it for something else it was: an excellent way to continue hanging out with racers after my own racing was done.

Because, when it comes right down to it, racers are the only kinds of folks I ever wanted to hang around with anyway.

# 7

# Fast Times

As a group, racers—and by that I mean drivers, mechanics and team owners—have always been wilder than folks in what I like to call the civilian world. I think that's true even now, despite the fact that the sponsorship and media demands of today's racing have turned a lot of top drivers into politically correct robots.

I feel bad for those guys because they don't get much of a chance to let their hair down and be themselves. Things were a whole bunch different in the 1960s and '70s. Back then race drivers acted the way I believe all race drivers would act naturally if they got the chance.

Meaning this: They were crazy.

*Gary Rovazzini: Simpson had a home on the beach in California, and I went to a couple of parties there. I remember that when you first walked into the place you saw one of those water coolers, the kind with the big five-gallon bottle on top. Well, he sure didn't have water in it. He had a special concoction he'd mixed up—rum and whatever else, with some Kool-Aid or something in there to make it sweet. Whenever you walked by, you'd fill your cup, and it didn't take too many of those before you were pretty well wiped out. I can remember Simpson and Jerry Grant shooting machine guns off outside. I never figured out what that was about. In those days we partied hard.*

Whenever we had some time off from racing, we didn't waste it.

We were crazy seven days a week, crazy 24 hours a day, just plain crazy. It was a wonderful time to be alive. Anybody who was around back then—Indy car racer, drag racer, NASCAR racer, it doesn't matter—will tell you the same thing.

> **Parnelli Jones:** *I think the reason racers are so mischievous is that they spend so much time in a dangerous business, and in the back of their minds they know about the possibilities that are out there—possibilities of getting hurt, or worse. That makes you live the rest of your life with a little extra bit of gusto, I think. What I'm getting at, I guess, is that most race drivers tend to be hell-raisers.*

> **Don Prudhomme:** *What brought on all that craziness? Hell, it's pretty damn easy: When you got into racing, especially when we did, you lived on the edge and you knew it. And when you live like that, you need a release. So you go out and have some drinks and throw some parties and one thing leads to another. And maybe there's something else, too: When you race and you do it well, you think you're bigger than life.*

We certainly did live on the edge. I mean, racing today is still dangerous, but it's nothing like it was back then. Let's face it, the old cliché is true—you knew every weekend that somebody in your crowd might get killed. So I'm sure that subconsciously we all thought, Hell, I'm going to live it up tonight, because in two weeks I might not be around.

Those were fast times, buddy, and I had the best seat in the house for the whole ride. In those days my fun train had no caboose.

Across 16th Street from the Indianapolis Motor Speedway was a bar called The Cave. It was a real dive, but I was very attracted to this one girl who worked there; she was just a fine, fine woman. I hit on her every time I was in town for four or five years, but I got nowhere.

One night she said to me, "Look, I'll go out with you when you qualify for that race across the street."

I filed away that information and carried it around with me. Finally, in 1974, I qualified for the 500. That same night I walked into The Cave and said, "Honey, I'm in the race."

She said, "I heard. I get off work at two o'clock."

At two in the morning we left The Cave and she drove me to a little town west of Indianapolis. We pulled into this nice, tidy subdivision, the kind of neighborhood that looked like a postcard for family life instead of some place a single barmaid might live.

I said, "Uh, you're not married, are you?"

She said, "Don't worry about a thing."

Which, hindsight tells me, wasn't exactly a strong denial. But I listened to her and I stopped worrying. Even when we got into the house and I noticed some strange things—a guy's boots in the corner, stuff like that—I didn't think twice. That went against my best survival instincts, but I have a good explanation: Every red-blooded male knows that pretty women can make you stupid.

Anyway, I relaxed. That turned out to be a mistake because as soon as we settled into the bedroom and things started to get interesting, I heard a door slam at the other end of the house. Next I heard footsteps coming down the hallway. Then all the lights went on and I saw this massive guy standing there. I mean, this dude took up the whole doorway.

I figured I was dead, but it never hurts to try to talk your way out of a jam. I looked up and said, "Hey, man, it's OK. We haven't really done anything yet."

The guy turned on his heels and stomped off down the hall. All I could figure was, This sonofabitch is going for a gun! I grabbed my clothes, held them out in front of me, and jumped right through the bedroom window without even stopping to open it. It was just bang, smash, crash and out. Thank God it was a first-floor bedroom.

I hauled ass down the street, running for my life. I never even slowed down long enough to put on my pants. Better naked and running, I figured, than fully clothed and dead. And then, like a miracle, I saw a car up ahead with red lights on top: the local cops. Never in my life had I been so happy to see a lawman.

I ran up to the car and the cop was shaking his head. Clearly, it wasn't every night that he saw a naked guy sprinting through that neighborhood with his jeans in his hand.

The cop said, "There's *got* to be an explanation for this."

I said, "Yeah, there is. See, I qualified for the Indy 500 today, and there was this chick. . . ."

He listened to my tale, told me to get dressed and drove me back to the Speedway Motel. I fell asleep thinking, There's one more bullet I dodged. And I made a mental note to avoid The Cave for a while.

That incident would have never taken place, of course, had it not been for the girl. That was typical in those days. Sometimes it seemed like our whole world revolved around women.

> **Bill Hildick:** *When I was doing that Norton deal, we took our show car up to one of our plants in Troy, New York. When we got there we found that they had put together kind of an open house, and it was hosted by a bunch of young women who actually worked for the company, doing book-keeping and things like that. Simpson thought one of those girls was the absolute living end. Big surprise, right? Anyway, that kind of put me on alert. Well, next thing I knew, we couldn't find Bill. I said to Rolla Vollstedt, "The last thing I want is to find out tomorrow morning that our driver has been out with one of these gals and gotten our whole program sideways." Vollstedt agreed.*
>
> *He and I went out in two different directions, looking through every nightclub we could find. Two hours later we were both back at the Holiday Inn, where we were all staying. Neither of us had seen any sign of Simpson. We're standing there, wondering what to do next, and Vollstedt*

*says, "Let's check the hotel bar." So we go walking into the*
*Holiday Inn bar, and there's Simpson with all those girls.*

*When we told him we'd been out looking for him, Simp-*
*son said, "Hey, I've been right here all along, doing what I'm*
*supposed to do: mingling with the employees."*

Looking back, I think there was a female behind every off-the-wall thing that happened then, to me or my friends.

In 1971 Steve Krisiloff and I lived together in a basement apartment in Indianapolis. It was a crazy time, which was OK because Krisiloff and I were both pretty crazy anyway.

**Steve Krisiloff:** *We were both at the bottom of the barrel,*
*just coming into the sport. We didn't know a whole bunch of*
*people in town and nobody cared about us. I mean, we were*
*the new guys, and the new guys didn't hang around with the*
*guys who had been around a while. It just didn't work that*
*way. So Simpson and I kinda found each other and we had a*
*good time together. Neither one of us was married then and*
*we just had a lot of fun.*

I also had a place out in California and Stevie came out once to see me. While he was out there he got hooked up with this girl who was the daughter of some wealthy surgeon. They went out a few times and eventually her family invited Krisiloff and me to dinner at their home in a high-dollar section of Los Angeles. That was cool because on our budgets a decent meal was a rarity.

There we were, in this huge dining room. The table sat about 20, but there were only seven or eight of us. There was an empty chair between me and Stevie, and we were getting ready to eat. All of a sudden, just as the food was being served, this big old dog came walking into the room and jumped into that empty chair. Come to find out it was *his* chair. The dog ate right at the goddam table!

He gobbled up all his food and licked his chops. Obviously he was still hungry. So he looked over at Krisiloff's food, made a quick lunge and gobbled that up too. Stevie was sitting there, stunned. Next thing I knew, the dog made a move for my food, but I wasn't having any of that. I smacked him, smacked him hard, and it knocked him right out of his chair. The host family got a little pissed off about that, but, hey, I was hungry, man. I wasn't about to turn the best meal I had seen in months over to some mutt.

Probably the most bizarre event in my racing life happened in 1971 and, yes, a woman was at the center of it all.

USAC scheduled an Indy car race on a new oval in Rafaela, Argentina. The promoters shipped the cars down there at no cost to the teams, and they also paid the air fare for the drivers and two or three mechanics per car. We flew in on two chartered Boeing 707s, both full of racers and officials, and landed at an air force base in Parana. We were escorted to one side of the airfield, where there was a chauffeured car and an interpreter waiting for every driver. From there they took us to Rafaela, where each of us had accommodations for the weekend in private homes; there weren't enough hotels in the area to house us all.

My little team—me, Larry Burton and Jim Ward—was placed in a household that had five daughters; I'd guess their ages ranged from 19 to 28. Their parents moved out for the weekend to make room for the visiting Americans . . . and left the daughters behind to see that we were taken care of. I thought I had died and gone to heaven.

That first night, I decided I wanted to go out on the town. I had my interpreter explain this to the girls, so we—the five sisters and me—went to a huge outdoor disco. I had one of the sisters out on the dance floor, doing the boogaloo, and through the crowd I spotted this woman, this absolutely gorgeous woman, standing against a wall.

I dragged the interpreter over there and had him tell her that I wanted to buy her a drink. She said something back to him and he looked at me a little bit funny.

I asked him, "What did the lady say?"

The interpreter hesitated. Then he said, "She says you are nothing but a monkey."

It wasn't the smoothest start, but it was still a start. She warmed up a bit and we attempted a conversation with her limited English and my limited Spanish. Language barrier or no language barrier, I was very impressed by her. Her name was Christina, she was a lawyer and she lived in the city of Santa Fé, which was about 40 miles away. I left the disco that night wanting very badly to see her again.

The next day I headed to the track, which was kind of a dreary place. There were these giant beetles everywhere, two or three inches long. They got into everything; when you rolled up the garage door in the morning you'd hear 'em popping and crunching in the runners. Dan Gurney's team was in the stall next to us and all I heard that first morning was Wayne Leary, Gurney's mechanic, muttering over and over, "These fuckin' beetles."

I was helping my guys unload our equipment when a USAC official came by with a bulletin: *All drivers are to report to the Jockey Club tonight at such-and-such time for some fancy welcoming party*. Well, I knew right away I wasn't going to be there. At that point in my life I wasn't interested in fancy welcoming parties. Besides, I had met this terrific lady and I wanted to spend more time with her. So, without saying anything to anybody, I just didn't go to the Jockey Club.

The next day the USAC brass was hot. They said, "Look, Bill, attending these affairs is part of your responsibility down here."

I said, "Hang on. On the entry blank it didn't explain what my responsibilities were. I entered my car in this race and that's why I'm here—to run the race. Unless you're going to start paying me by the hour, you don't have any say in how I spend my time away from the track."

Clearly, USAC and I were not going to have a pleasant vacation in South America. That grew more apparent when we got another bulletin: On the second night, we were all expected to be the guests of honor at a dinner held by the governor of the province. I skipped that one too, and hung out with Christina again.

This went on for four straight nights: Get an invitation, blow it off. I mean, I didn't show up for anything.

> **Larry Burton:** *Bill marched to his own drummer, which caused him a lot of problems in Argentina. The USAC people wanted him to go to this function and that function, and that just wasn't his deal.*

The way I saw it, things were pretty simple: These big politicians and socialites were not very appealing when you stacked them up against a pretty girl. By the time Sunday rolled around, I knew I was in big trouble with USAC because I was the only driver who wasn't showing up for these affairs. But it wasn't over yet.

We ran the race—Al Unser won it, Bentley Warren and Lloyd Ruby had a big fiery crash, and my car had an injector problem—and I took off for Santa Fé. I was crazy about this Argentine girl and I just had to be with her.

There was one last official bash, the awards dinner on Monday night, and then at 9:00 A.M. on Tuesday we were scheduled to depart from Parana on the two chartered planes. Well, the way I looked at it, I was in such deep shit already that it didn't make much sense to start behaving now. I said, "Screw the awards dinner. Screw the flight home. I'm going to hang out here in Argentina for a while."

Christina and I spent all day Monday together, and at nine on Tuesday, when I was due to be airborne, heading back to the States, we were fast asleep in a room at the Hotel Santa Fé.

There was a tiny problem I hadn't counted on. This was the height of the Juan Perón era, when Argentina was a police state. Everything was very regimented, done precisely by the book, and the air force wasn't about to let those chartered planes leave until everybody was accounted for. I hadn't ever considered that; I just figured those guys would fly off without me and I'd grab a commercial airline flight a week or so later. But the government down there was not about to get involved in some scandal involving a missing Indy car racer, so the order came down: The planes do not move until the head count is complete and accurate.

The USAC guys did a quick roll call, and naturally there was one idiot missing: Bill Simpson.

> ***Larry Burton:*** *I was sitting on that plane with [Indianapolis Motor Speedway owner] Tony Hulman and Henry Banks, from USAC, and they were giving me dirty looks. They kept asking me, 'Where's Simpson?' Hell, I didn't know. I told them, 'He's a big boy. He can find his own way home. Take off without him.' But they wouldn't.*

They gave my name to the local officials, and that triggered a manhunt, which actually took very little time. See, in a police state it's hard to move around unchecked if you're a foreigner. When you registered at a hotel you had to show your passport, and all that information was promptly turned over to the police. Once the news got around that they were searching for me, it was just a matter of cross-checking till some clerk said, "Hey, he's at the Hotel Santa Fé."

At about 10:30 A.M. there was a huge crash and the door of my hotel room flew off its hinges. It was the *federales*, the military police, and they were not happy. All I saw were guns, large guns. I jumped out of bed with my hands up; Christina was covering up on the bed, petrified. They told me to get dressed, then they dragged my fugitive ass downstairs and threw me into a car. Right behind me came Christina, half-dressed and jabbering away at the cops. She jumped into the car with me, they slammed the door behind her, and off we went, hauling ass to the air base. The whole time, Christina was hanging onto my arm, crying in her cute little accent, "No, Beel! Don't go, Beel!"

By the time we reached the air base, it was maybe 11 o'clock. The first thing I saw was our 707, still sitting on the ramp two hours after its scheduled take-off. Whatever trouble I had been in with USAC before, I knew it was nothing compared to this.

The cops escorted me up the stairs and into the airplane, and as I walked through the door there was a chorus of boos. If I had been a bit of an Indy car outsider before, I was definitely a bad guy now. Everybody was hollering and throwing stuff at me; I mean, they were really pissed off. They had a pretty good reason, by the way: It was about 100 degrees outside and there was no auxiliary power unit hooked up to the plane, which meant no air-conditioning. They had been sitting on that airliner for a couple of hours, roasting, because the cops and the soldiers didn't want to let anyone off for fear that another driver might slip away.

The best thing I could think of to say was, "Uh, sorry, guys."

It was not the smoothest ride home.

When I showed up at Phoenix for the next race, the registrar at the sign-in window said, "Bill, you have a problem." He sent me to see Frankie Delroy, and from there I was kicked up the USAC chain of command to Dick King, the assistant to the executive director, and finally to the executive director himself, Bill Smyth. I had a problem, all right: I had been fined $5,000 for my conduct in Argentina. In 1971 five grand was a huge pile of money.

I said, "What exactly am I being fined for?"

First they told me the official reason was "FBAA." I asked what that meant and they replied, "For Being an Asshole." Then they said it was because my conduct in Argentina was un-American, which was bullshit. The way I figured it, if anyone had acted un-American down there it was the USAC big shots, and I told them so. I said, "You guys spent the entire week wining and dining the upper echelon of Argentine society. I was out every night, mixing with the common people, being a good ambassador."

Not surprisingly, the folks from the United States Auto Club did not share my view. They told me not to unload my car until I paid the fine, so I did the only thing I could do: I wrote them a check. I didn't bother to inform them that there was no money in the account. The check got me into the race, and by the first part of the following week I had the money in place to make it good.

The punch line to the whole Argentina story is that I ended up marrying Christina. We had stayed in touch after my grand exit from Parana and I visited her whenever I could. She finally came to America on the eve of the 1974 Indy 500. She watched me run that race and then the two of us flew to California and stayed for about six weeks on my boat, which was docked at the Portofino Hotel in Redondo Beach.

One day I was standing on deck, with Christina down below. These two well-dressed guys showed up, both of them obviously South American. They said to me, "Are you Mr. Simpson?" I nodded and they gave me a peek at the nice pistols they happened to be carrying. They told me they were taking Christina back to Argentina. Her father, who was a pretty well-connected politician, had decided as a matter of honor that he didn't want her living this way anymore.

I said, "I don't want her to leave. How can we rectify this?"

They said, "Well, you can marry her."

I poked my head below deck and said, "Christina, we've got to go. We're getting married."

We went into Santa Monica and got a marriage license, but in those days you had to wait three days before the ceremony. So we waited, all four of us—me, Christina, and the two guys with the guns. Once we were married, they took off and my new wife and I went back to the Portofino.

Speaking of the Portofino, that place played a pretty large role in my life back then. Even before Christina came along, I was basically living right there at the marina.

> **Tom McEwen:** *Simpson always had a boat tied up in the harbor. Sometimes he could afford it and sometimes he couldn't, but he always had one.*

The Portofino was owned by Mary Davis, a great lady who was also tough enough to eat nails for breakfast. The manager, Phil Martinez, was a die-hard racing guy; he spent several years moonlighting at various jobs for Goodyear at the bigger Indy car races, just to be around the scene.

My Portofino days were kind of wild. For better or worse, there was always something going on.

One Friday I went with three of my buddies up to Marina del Rey, where we drank until the bars closed. Everybody picked up a girl except me; it was just one of those bad nights. When there was nothing left to do, these three couples and I headed back to the Portofino on my sailboat, the appropriately named *Ship of Fools*. It was a 12-mile cruise, straight south. Everybody else headed below deck and I was at the helm. Well, it was colder than hell, so I grabbed a bottle of Scotch to keep me warm. This might not sound like a bright idea, slugging straight Scotch at the helm of a sailboat at night, but it made sense at the time.

By the time we got close to the Portofino, I was blind drunk. It didn't help matters any that it was a very foggy night. I made the big turn into the marina and started inching along, feeling my way home. I saw a channel that looked like the right way to my slip and swung the boat in that direction. God, was that ever a wrong turn.

At the end of that channel was the Portofino's Sea Bucket restaurant, with its big glass windows four or five feet beyond the dock's concrete wall. Well, *Ship of Fools* had an eight-foot bowsprit, which is the correct term for those long poles you see on the front end of sailboats. You can do the math on your own. I heard a horrendous noise, glass breaking everywhere. Then I felt this tremendous thud and the boat just stopped.

I knew something big had happened, but I was too stunned and too drunk to take it all in. Through the fog I heard the voice of another marina resident, my friend Bob Hayward. He climbed onto my boat, backed it away and drove it into its proper slip. My pals and their women all staggered off to wherever they went and I headed down to my stateroom and passed out.

The next morning at first light there was a giant commotion outside my boat. It was Mary Davis: "Simpson, you sonofabitch, get your ass out of bed and look at what you did to my restaurant!"

That's when everything became clear. My bowsprit had knocked out the windows and pushed in all the dockside booths. The booths smashed into the counter, and the counter tipped over and hit the back wall, and the whole back wall tipped forward. I mean, the entire restaurant was caved in, trashed.

I was not the most popular guy at the Portofino for a while. Mary wanted to throw me out of the marina for good, but Phil Martinez, just because he was a racing buddy of mine, talked her into giving me a break and letting me stay.

Boats, I discovered, were like race cars: They could give you a few headaches, but they could be a lot of fun too.

> **Chris Karamesines:** *One time Simpson had a brand-new boat there in Redondo Beach. He was going away on a trip, so I asked him if I could use it. He said, 'Fine, go ahead.' While he was gone we renamed it in my honor. We had 'The Greek Tycoon, Chicago, Illinois' painted right across the back. Everybody around there just figured Simpson had gotten in trouble and had to sell the boat.*

In 1979 I was one of three guys who chartered a yacht called the *Jolly Roger* and parked it in the Monte Carlo harbor for the Grand Prix of Monaco. My two partners in the deal were my friend Dave Russell, from Russell Performance Products, and a guy named Douglas Morton, whom we had met through Rupert Keegan, the Formula One driver. Dougie was a hell of an interesting guy who was literally a soldier of fortune; he made a pile of money working around the world as a mercenary soldier.

Hanging around Morton could scare you a little bit. We were sitting around one night, drinking and telling stories about the lives we had led. I told a couple about racing and chasing women. Dougie told one about being hired to get rid of some general in a Third World country whose name I can't remember. What I do remember is how he explained that whole mission. He said he strung some fish-net material down the side of a narrow road for about a quarter-mile, then ran it across the road and back up the other side. Every 25 yards or so he attached to the fishnet a five-gallon can of gasoline and a grenade, rigged so that the pin would come out once the net-ting was pulled hard. Pretty soon here came this caravan of cars with the general in it. When the driver of the lead car spotted that fishnet strung across the road, his natural reaction was to speed up and try to bust right through it. That, of course, sucked the rest of the netting right around the trailing cars. The grenades and the gasoline took care of things from there.

By the time he got to the end of that story, I decided to stay on the good side of Douglas Morton.

Later, in London, I was with him and a beautiful lady friend of his named Yolanda, and the three of us hailed a cab. Dougie opened the door and Yolanda got in first. Well, before we could climb in behind her, this other guy came up, jumped in from the other side and yelled for the cabbie to take off. Dougie was running down the street, punching at the back window as the cab pulled away. The other guy was sitting inside, giving Dougie the finger. All I could think was, That fellow has no idea who he's messing with. He just stole the girlfriend of a guy who eliminates generals.

So Dave and Doug and I had the *Jolly Roger* in Monaco. One day we threw a big party at lunch time. We had a bunch of people on board, with a crew of seven taking care of everybody. It was a real happening. We had Saudi princes partying with us and all kinds of major and minor celebrities. George Hamilton, the actor, tried to come on board, but Dougie Morton apparently didn't like Hamilton's movies, so that was that. Access denied.

I was mingling around, talking to our guests, when I looked up and saw Jackie Stewart, the three-time World Driving Champion, standing there with four long-haired guys. Maybe you know their names: John Lennon, Paul McCartney, George Harrison, Ringo Starr.

The Beatles. On our boat.

I mean, I wasn't necessarily a Beatles fan, but the band had broken up 10 years earlier and it was a pretty big deal for them to be anywhere together. I probably should have hung out with them a little bit more, but I was too busy having fun.

That particular Monaco weekend was a nonstop party. We skipped over to a yacht belonging to Adnan Khashoggi, the Saudi arms dealer who was reputed to be one of the wealthiest men in the world. His yacht was about 180 feet long, with four levels. There were people everywhere, drinking champagne and doing what you do at parties, which back then meant just about anything. One of the top Formula One drivers of the day started romancing this beautiful girl and before you know it the two of them were upstairs in one of the staterooms, making love. Two problems: The guy had a wife; and she was downstairs at the party. Eventually the wife wondered what had become of the husband and set off to look for him. In the course of wandering throughout the ship she came to this stateroom and heard a familiar voice inside. She threw open the door and caught her husband, shall we say, in the act.

The guy was in big trouble and he knew it. But, like me, he subscribed to the theory that it never hurts to try to talk your way out. I'm thankful for that because in the process he came up with one of the greatest lines I've ever heard. He looked over his shoulder at his wife, looked back down at the naked girl on the bed, then turned to his wife and screamed, "Honey, I thought this was *you!*"

I'll tell you, my brief time hanging around those Formula One guys was a riot.

One night we were in a disco—I'll leave the country nameless, because who can tell about international statutes of limitations?—and I was pretty well sloshed. I got a phone call from a racing journalist who knew we were there. He said, "Bill, you must come to Trixie's." Well, I was out with a bunch of folks—a team manager, another top Formula One racer, a prominent sponsor. I told this guy I had some people with me. He said, "You must bring your friends and come to Trixie's."

I said, "How do I get there?"

He said, "Get in any taxi. The driver will know."

So we grabbed a taxi and I announced, "We want to go to Trixie's." The driver laughed a little bit and we headed out of town.

It soon became clear why the taxi driver had chuckled. Trixie's was what some people might call a house of pleasure and what I would call an old-fashioned whorehouse. The lady in charge welcomed us, but she wasn't too excited about me being as drunk as I was. I can't blame her because I was definitely wobbly-wheeled. She sent my buddies off with some of her girls and told me, "You go and wait in that room down the hall."

I walked into this dusty old room and sat down on the bed. In hindsight I can see that she sent me in there to dry out, but at the time I was sure a pretty girl was going to walk in at any minute. I got naked fast. When no pretty girl showed up after a period of time, I started hollering, "Send a girl down here!"

None showed up. I hollered again. Still no girl. So I modified my command a bit: "Send a girl down here right now or I'm going to burn this place down!"

It was only an empty threat, just a drunk mouthing off. But as soon as I said it, I saw a pack of matches sitting on the table. Just to amuse myself, I lit one match and held it out toward the drapes, as if to say, "I mean it! I'm going to burn this place down!"

Well, when the match got close to that dusty curtain, it went up like an incendiary bomb. The entire room was a wall of fire in a matter of seconds. I had about a hundred drinks in me, but now, naked in a blazing room, I was suddenly as sober as a judge. I grabbed my clothes and ran down the hall, yelling, "Guys, we've got to get out of here! The place is on fire!"

My buddies didn't believe me at first, but they caught on fast. Maybe the smoke was the tip-off, I don't know. Anyway, here went all these prominent Formula One folks, half-dressed, running out into the street, followed by all the working girls. The ladies stood there and watched the blaze. My friends and I did not. By the time we got to the end of the block, Trixie's was well on its way to burning completely to the ground.

Foolish? Of course. Careless? Certainly. But that was the way a lot of us lived for a long time. Once you adopted that old '60s-style racer's philosophy—live it up tonight because in two weeks you might not be around—it was hard to shake. The times had changed, but we hadn't.

I'm not saying it was the right way to look at things, but you've got to remember that we'd all seen, up close, just how fleeting life could be. So instead of walking around in a constant state of dread that something might go wrong, and instead of mourning when something *did* go wrong, we just stood on the gas harder.

When my friend Mike Sarokin was killed, in 1968, my reaction was not what normal folks might call typical. I boarded an airline flight to Australia, just looking to get away for a while. When the plane stopped to refuel in Fiji, in the South Pacific, I got off and went for a walk. And I just kept walking. The flight left for Australia without me and I could not have cared less.

Fiji handles a pretty good number of tourists today, but back in '68 it was a whole lot less civilized. One of the English-speaking locals told me about a village where there was turmoil because the only power source, a generator, had stopped working. I said, "Hell, I can fix a generator." He walked me down the dirt roads until we found the village, where I saw this diesel generator just sitting there, silent. I messed around with it a bit and the only thing I could find wrong was that there was a bunch of water in the fuel. I got the lines cleaned out, dumped in some fresh fuel and fired that sucker up.

Well, when that thing came to life, those people just about made me their king. They had a big party and we all got drunk on some kind of homemade grog they brewed up. In the middle of the night they stopped everything and held a ceremony; they had me jump over a log, which somehow meant I was married to the village leader's daughter. I ended up partying on Fiji for two weeks. And then I caught a flight back home.

It was a strange way to handle the death of a close friend, but it was the only way I knew. Maybe you had to be around during that time to fully appreciate what I mean.

Art Pollard, who was killed in a practice crash at Indianapolis in '73, was another pretty good friend of mine. Like the rest of us, he enjoyed the race driver's life. Like the rest of us, it got him in trouble sometimes. On the day of his crash Art and I were talking in Gasoline Alley and he told me he had gotten engaged to two women.

I said, "Art, that's not good, being engaged to two girls at once. What are you going to do?"

He said, "I guess I'm going to have to pick one, huh?"

To this day I have no idea whether he was serious about any of this. But I'll never forget what happened next.

Just joking around, Art said, "I probably ought to just go out there and bust my ass. You know, kill myself."

Ten minutes later he was dead.

Like I said, those were fast times.

# 8

# Ups and Downs

I started looking into manufacturing helmets in 1973, after I was knocked out in my giant crash at Indianapolis in Rolla Vollstedt's car. That was the most serious whack on the head I had ever taken, and it gave me all the reason I needed to start looking at the downside of head injuries.

At that time there were several companies building helmets, the best-known being Bell and Premier. I never felt like they made *bad* helmets, but I did feel like their line of thinking—hell, the entire industry's line of thinking—was outdated. The typical helmet they sold to a race driver was essentially a motorcycle lid, just something hard to keep you from smashing your head open if you fell off your Harley. The problem was, those helmets didn't dissipate a lot of energy; while the outside of your head might come out of a crash intact, the shock of the impact was transferred right to the brain. I felt it would be better for the helmet itself to absorb the brunt of the impact, in the same way that a race car that bends a bit in a crash is safer than one that is absolutely rigid.

The way I saw it, this kind of helmet would help everybody. If it would let us walk away from big crashes at places like the Speedway, it would clearly be safer for motorcycle riders too.

I went to Roy Richter, who was still running Bell, and told him what I thought he ought to be doing. Roy listened to what I had to say and agreed with my concept. Right away he got Bell started on a program to rethink the way it built its helmets. Unfortunately, business intervened. Roy sold Bell to a large corporation and everything changed. A short time later, someone from the new group told me they were not interested in this philosophy Roy and I were pursuing; in fact they'd already terminated three or four employees who were designing the kinds of helmets Roy and I had discussed.

That situation bothered me a great deal. Under Roy Richter Bell had done a lot of really neat things. They came up with the first full-face helmet and some pretty nice helmet liners using expanded-bead Styrene, plus a few more tricks. But it was clear to me that this new corporate ownership didn't care much about things like that. These guys were, plain and simple, just a bunch of suits keeping an eye on the company's bottom line.

I thought long and hard about that and in the end I decided to go into the helmet business myself. I hired the folks Bell had decided weren't of any value any more and I also hired a fellow named Luciano Aguirre, who had worked for Premier. He went to work for me on Normandy Avenue, in Torrance, in a place that was nothing but a ten-by-ten-foot room, where we got our helmet division rolling.

Before long we were building a prototype of a Simpson helmet, and in the spring of '74 I wore the first one ever to see competition. By today's standards it was nothing special, but back then it was a pretty neat piece, much lighter than anything else a guy could wear.

Al Unser looked at my helmet and liked it enough to order one for himself. He got it in time for an Indy car race at the old Texas World Speedway, and it's probably a good thing he did. Al had a terrible crash in turn one; he hit so violently that his new helmet left a white streak on the wall—a streak maybe 400 feet long. It was clear that he had smacked his head pretty good, yet Al was never knocked out. The other drivers saw that and here came an avalanche of orders for our helmets.

As the next several years passed, we had a few other drivers unwillingly put our headgear to the test. At Phoenix, in 1981, Johnny Rutherford flipped Jim Hall's Chaparral on the front stretch and landed literally on his head. The car's roll hoop held up fine, but Rutherford's helmet was banging and scraping against the asphalt. I mean, he just tore up the outside of that helmet.

*Johnny Rutherford: There is no doubt in my mind that Bill's helmet saved my life. That helmet took a tremendous beating; in fact, the Snell Foundation, which does all the testing and certification of racing helmets, was amazed to find a helmet that had been subjected to so much destructive force without producing a fatal injury. The last paragraph of the Snell report said that a helmet of any less integrity would have almost certainly produced a fatality.*

*Dick Berggren: I spent time with Bill once as he crash-tested some helmets. He had devised a piece of equipment that was basically a weight he would drop onto a helmet, and inside the helmet he had a sensor that would determine the effects of that impact on the wearer. With the help of that sensor he was able to develop better helmets, in terms of both the inner liner and the shell itself.*

Getting into the helmet business led to an interesting by-product. It meant that unlike a lot of companies that specialized in, say, suits or shoes or seat belts, the Simpson logo could now be found on just about everything relating to a driver's safety, from head to toe. That wasn't my intent; I just wanted to make better helmets than the next guy was making. But offering a complete line of safety gear made our company bigger, stronger, more of a key player in the racing game.

As it turned out, getting bigger had its minuses too. It allowed me to see first-hand all the aggravations a major business can bring.

Right from the beginning, our competitors in the safety field have provided some of my biggest headaches. It's not that I don't like competition; that's the American way, and each time my company expanded into a different field it had to compete with whoever was already there. I think we always did it fairly. We let other companies do their thing, we did our thing, and we figured that if our thing was a bit better, it would catch on. In any business that's how you pay your dues, and I feel like I've paid mine.

I have never had a problem with any company that has operated by those guidelines. The way I see it, if your firm competes with mine and that competition involves a fair battle between your ideas and my ideas, that's cool. But if your company wants to get into the game without paying its dues, and just wants to make a buck by trying to sell someone else's ideas as its own, that's a different story. And too much of that goes on every day in the racing safety business.

In my opinion very few of the other safety companies have ever shown a desire to innovate, to push things forward the way we have. What some of them choose to do instead is copy any idea they think is a good one, slap a Brand X label on it and sell it as their own. This may sound like a self-serving overstatement, but I mean it sincerely. In the past 15 years there have only been a couple of major advances in the safety business that didn't originate on a Simpson drawing board. Every single product we have made has been copied, usually by at least three or four manufacturers. I'll bet our high-top racing shoe alone has been copied by seven or eight of our competitors.

I get asked all the time how I feel about that and I won't lie to you: It pisses me off. It pisses me off because it takes no great amount of brains or ingenuity to copy something, and because a simple copy contributes nothing toward making this sport safer.

People talk about imitation being the most sincere form of flattery. Well, I don't feel flattered when I see a rival company's name on something that is just a dead-ass copy of a product we developed. Should I take it as a compliment when we spend months of time and thousands of dollars perfecting an idea and someone else copies it in a matter of days and spends next to nothing?

Here is the problem with our industry today: If you've got enough money to buy a couple of industrial sewing machines, you can be selling fire suits or gloves or flame-resistant underwear in two weeks. You might not have any idea what you're doing and you might not understand the science behind any of this, but that doesn't matter as long as you can take reasonably accurate measurements and

When you spend an entire month at one track, the way we did at Indianapolis, you have a lot of downtime. But it's not exactly relaxing; the wait for the next practice session, and then for qualifying, and then for the race, is nerve-wracking. (*John Mahoney photo*)

The greatest moment in my racing life was starting the 1974 Indianapolis 500. This, then, must have been the second greatest. I've just finished my qualifying run. If I look a little puzzled, here's why: On the one hand I was elated because after four years of trying I had finally earned a starting position in the biggest race in the world; on the other hand I was thinking, Well, you're here—now what? I guess any driver who qualifies for his first 500 feels those butterflies. (*Photo courtesy Indianapolis Motor Speedway*)

Early in 1974 I ran the California 500, at the old Ontario Motor Speedway, in this ancient Brabham. The car belonged to John Martin, the engine was borrowed from A.J. Watson and Bob Wilke, and we had a small amount of backing from a bar called Apple Annie's Speakeasy. Nobody gave us a shot to make the race, but we did, and we clawed our way to 14th at the finish. That weekend went a long way toward boosting my morale, which had sunk pretty low after the previous couple of years. (*Bill Simpson Collection*)

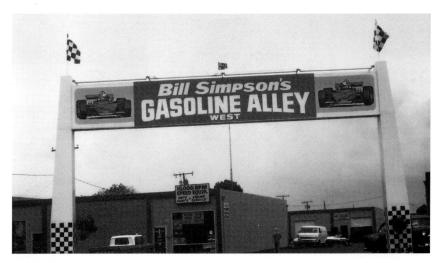

In the 1970s I built a small industrial complex on Normandy Avenue in Torrance, California. I called it Gasoline Alley West, and I wouldn't rent you a shop there unless you had some connection to racing. Back then that was easy, because Southern California was home to a ton of Indy car, sprint car, midget and drag-racing people. I still have the property; one of our Simpson World stores is there, as are a couple of hot-rod and custom motorcycle fabricators and an off-road team. (*Bill Simpson Collection*)

Here's a little history: The long-haired guy on the left is me. The long-haired guy on the right is Rick Mears, getting ready to make the first Indy car start of his life, aboard my old Eagle, in the 1976 California 500. Today Rick is a four-time Indianapolis 500 winner, a three-time CART champion and one of my best friends. (*Bill Simpson Collection*)

My role as an advisor to the old Toyota pro-am celebrity series put me in the company of some awfully interesting people. That's me talking to the entertainer Paul Williams; on the far right is Fred Dryer, who used to play football for the Los Angeles Rams and later became an actor. (*Bill Simpson Collection*)

Dan Gurney is a guy I've respected for as long as I've known him. He's a good friend and also one of the greatest race drivers this country has ever produced. That's Christina and me chumming around with Dan back in the late '70s. (*Bill Simpson Collection*)

I had some good successes driving in those Toyota celebrity events. Here I am with my second wife, Christina, after a win at Watkins Glen. That was a fun day. (*Bill Simpson Collection*)

My post-driving days have included several ventures as a car
owner, including a brief Busch
Series effort with my son Dave
as the driver. Here he is, at
Daytona International Speedway, sporting number 38, which
I often ran on my Indy cars.
(*Bill Simpson Collection*)

In the late '80s I participated in a series of races at Indianapolis Raceway Park for "senior" drivers, in Jaguar sports cars. That's Johnny Rutherford in the middle and Bobby Unser on the right. Even though it was just a fun deal, it was still kind of thrilling to be in company like that. (*Bill Simpson Collection*)

For long stretches in the 1970s and '80s I lived on my boat in a marina in Redondo Beach. One weekend, while I was out of town, I lent the boat to Chris "The Golden Greek" Karamesines, a legendary drag racer and an old buddy of mine. When I got back I found the boat re-named in his honor and these two girls aboard. It was a pretty good joke, though I was mad at Greek for not getting me a blonde. (*Bill Simpson Collection*)

I've always enjoyed seeing young guys come along, especially the ones who show the same kind of raw hunger for driving race cars that I had when I was their age. Every generation has a few outstanding kids: Today there's Dale Earnhardt Jr. and Tony Stewart; in the '90s there were guys like Jeff Gordon, P.J. and Page Jones, and Davey Hamilton. In the early '80s Michael Andretti was one of those kids. Back when this photo was taken, Michael and I were both in Super Vees; I was a team owner and he was a driver. (*Bill Simpson Collection*)

Boats have always been a big thing with me; any time I can get out on the water these days, I'm there. Here's my grandson, Dillon, cruising around with me on Lake Norman in North Carolina. (*Bill Simpson Collection*)

In May of 2000 I was back in Gasoline Alley as an entrant in the Indianapolis 500, this time as a team co-owner. From left to right: my old pal Wayne Leary, me, co-owners Usona Purcell and Preston Root, and driver Andy Hillenburg and his wife Michelle. We didn't do as well as we'd hoped—we started 33rd and finished 28th, after a wheel bearing let us down—but we had a bunch of fun. (*Photo courtesy Indianapolis Motor Speedway*)

We might have started work on this book only in 1999, but you might say we've been doing the research for years. Here's me with my coauthor, Bones Bourcier, at a little party I held back in 1995 at my North Carolina lake house. (*Bourcier collection*)

Here's something that makes me feel good whenever I visit a Saturday-night short track: This guy, like so many others these days, has the latest suit, belts, gloves and neck collar. Sure, I'm glad he chose our brand, but mostly I'm glad that these grassroots guys now take safety more seriously than they used to. (*Dick Berggren Photo*)

When I met Dale Earnhardt, back in 1978, he was just a badass racer struggling to find his way. He's not struggling anymore, but I can assure you Earnhardt is still a badass. What I liked about him from day one was that he was more interested in being the best racer he could be than in all the other BS that went along with being a hero driver. Because of that, he got a reputation as being hard to get along with, but we've always had a great relationship, personally and professionally. He's been a loyal Simpson wearer for years. Earnhardt races for all the right reasons, and I respect that. (*Fr. Dale Grubba Photo*)

The quest for improved personal safety gear never stops. I've been tinkering with different methods of arresting the forward movement of a driver's head in a violent crash, something the industry hadn't seriously addressed until the last couple of years. (*Dick Berggren photo*)

Continually improving personal safety gear is not the only way to make racing safer. For several years now, I've been exploring the "soft-wall" concept. The concrete retaining walls we see at most tracks have proven to be too unforgiving, especially as speeds have climbed. Rather than absorbing impact, they transfer it back to the car and, ultimately, the driver. At the 2000 Brickyard 400 at Indianapolis, I had a small section of my own soft-wall system on hand, and it got a lot of attention from the NASCAR drivers.
(*Dick Berggren photo*)

make yourself a pattern. All you've got to do is buy something with a Simpson label, copy it as best you can, and call it your own.

I can't tell you how many times I've seen my people bust their butts to design something—go through all the necessary research and development and figure out a way to bring it to market at a fair price—only to have some sonofabitch come along and copy it. And the most galling thing of all is they always undercut your price by a few dollars and tell the racer he's getting a bargain.

Well, here's what I think of that: Give me any manufactured product in the world and I'll figure out a way to copy it and sell it cheaper than the original. The reason for that is simple: The guy who sold the first one based his price around what he spent to design, build, and develop the thing, while the guy who sells a copy avoids all of those expenses. But that doesn't mean that the cheap copy is worth a damn, because it almost certainly wasn't built with the same degree of care and know-how that went into the original.

I've heard racers rationalize their purchase of what I consider to be inferior safety gear by saying things like, "Simpson's price is higher." Well, when you're spending a million goddam dollars a year in R&D trying to find better ways to keep these guys alive, your stuff is bound to cost a few bucks more.

If I lose a customer to these copycat companies, I'm not happy about that, but it won't change my basic feelings on all of this. I'm not about to start copying what anybody else does, period. That goes against my grain.

Now, what I *have* done on occasion is look at something and say, "Hey, that seems like a good basic idea. How can we make it better?" That's quite a bit different—and a lot more difficult—than simply stealing a design. I'll go to someone who specializes in that particular area and we'll do the necessary research, and *then* we'll try to introduce a product that may be similar in concept but is better and safer in execution.

One example of that is the air-bottle system we use in drag racing, which gives a Funny Car driver four minutes of what is called "hospital air" in a bad fire. It was based on a system I saw elsewhere. I loved the idea, but I thought the application was kind of primitive. I took one of those units to a firm that made air bottles for firemen, who have to spend time in blazing, smoky buildings, and I said, "Look, here's the problem these drag racers are facing and here's what's available to them right now. Help me make this better."

By combining their ideas and our own, we improved on that system significantly. And, hopefully, Funny Car racers are safer because of our effort.

To me that's fair competition in this business. Had we gone out and simply copied that existing air system, it would surely have been cheaper and easier, and I'm sure that thanks to the name recognition our company has, we could have sold a ton of those things. But the level of safety in Funny Car racing would not have been advanced one inch and I wouldn't have been satisfied with that.

It bothers me that I can name any number of safety companies that don't share my philosophy. I don't have an ounce of respect for any of them and I never will. I don't feel like they've put anything back into this sport; they all take, take, take, selling as much of their knock-off stuff as they can, but none of them actually does a damn thing about making racing a safer sport. I have a deep, deep dislike for some of these people.

And yet, as big a headache as these other companies have given me, they've actually been only a minor distraction compared to the biggest single nuisance I have faced in my time in this business: the American legal system.

Anyone old enough to read a newspaper or watch television is aware of how lawsuit-happy this country has become. Well, I don't think anyone alive can tell you more about that topic than I can. When you make your living on the riskiest end of a risky business, you leave yourself open to all sorts of attacks from ambulance-chasing lawyers and their greedy clients. And sometimes it feels like I've met them all.

*Dick Berggren: For a while, a lot of racers who got hurt seemed to think it was just a golden opportunity to get rich. The manufacturers of safety equipment were getting their socks sued off.*

*David Lawson, longtime friend: Unfortunately for Simpson, he's in the kind of business where you can be hammered continually by people who get hurt and want to sue you. For a long time it seemed like even when he won those cases he lost, just because of the attorneys' fees and that kind of crap.*

*Rick Mears: Over the years I'd hear Bill comment about being sued for this and sued for that. I could never imagine being in that type of business, where you're dealing with this all the time. I mean, all he's done is try to make things better and safer, and here he'd be, getting sued. That has to wear thin real quick.*

From 1978 to '82 I helped Toyota organize its pro-celebrity races at Long Beach and Watkins Glen. My part of the deal was to help select the talent and then to train the movie actors, rock stars and athletes who made up the amateur end of the series. We'd go to Willow Springs and spend a few days teaching them about their safety gear and about how to drive fast without busting their asses. Then, on race weekends, I'd also compete; in fact I was fortunate enough to win two of those events.

For the most part it was a lot of fun. I got to hang out with actors like Gene Hackman and Clint Eastwood, musicians like Ted Nugent and Paul Williams, athletes like Joe Montana and Lynn Swann. They were nice people and I got sort of friendly with a few of them. Hackman and I hung out together for a while and got to know each other pretty well. And Nugent was a guy I liked because he was absolutely nuts. He sent me a Christmas card that showed a bloody Santa Claus lying dead in the snow and Ted standing there, his foot on Santa's chest and a hunting rifle in his hand.

Some of those celebrities, incidentally, might have been terrific drivers had they chosen that path. To this day I am amazed by the hand-eye coordination I found in Lynn Swann; it was easy to see why he was a Hall of Fame receiver in the National Football League.

Of course there's always one bad apple in every bunch, and in the case of these pro-celebrity races it was a fellow known as Fabian. Maybe you remember him: He was a singer who came out of Philadelphia in the late '50s and was a big heartthrob with the ladies in the teen-idol era. Fabian showed up at Willow Springs and it was clear from the start that he didn't want to listen to me or anybody else. I didn't like that, but I did my best to help him anyway. When it came time for him to take a few practice laps we climbed into one of the modified Toyota Celicas that were used in the series. Fabian was strapped into the driver's seat with a helmet and I was in the passenger seat with no safety gear but a seat belt, because this was supposed to be an acclimation session, not a flat-out, high-speed run. Well, instead he went flying down the back straightaway, hard on the throttle, and when we got to turn eight he just refused to lift.

I knew we were going to crash long before Fabian did. I hollered at him to back off and when that didn't work I reached over and hit him in the neck as hard as I could. That got his foot off the gas, but by that point it was too late. We went sailing off the track, a wheel dug into the dirt, and we went end-for-end. By the time we stopped, that damn car was all but broken in half. The windshield had flown out, so I crawled out through the opening and went around to grab Fabian, who was in shock. The wreck had scared the hell out of him, which I could understand because it scared the hell out of me too.

To make a long story short, he ended up suing me, suing Toyota, suing the Willow Springs track, suing *everybody* for negligence of one kind or another. It was a bullshit suit from the word go, in my opinion, but I took it very seriously.

The case was heard in Torrance. The courtroom was always

packed with spectators because I brought in a bunch of athletes and movie stars to testify on my behalf. I had to prove I wasn't some reckless cowboy who had put the great Fabian in danger; I was a professional whose job it was to help keep this jerk from killing himself.

The whole thing was so ridiculous that by the time the jury came back, they had big grins on their faces. They gave Fabian nothing. In fact they actually wanted to know if they could award *me* some money, because I had sustained a broken cheekbone and a broken nose and because I had put myself in danger by climbing back into the wreckage to rescue this guy.

The only positive side of the whole Fabian mess was that, in the end, common sense prevailed.

I had a similar favorable result in a case involving a guy who crashed a sports car and had a terrible fire at Riverside in the late '60s, but this time I had to go a pretty long way to prove my case.

This fellow had climbed out of the wreck OK, but apparently he was disoriented from the impact and ended up staggering around in the flames for something like 40 or 50 seconds. We knew this because someone had captured everything on 8-millimeter film. The guy got burned pretty good, especially on his legs, and he subsequently sued me. This was a weird case, because he didn't sue anybody else. Normally everybody even peripherally involved in these things gets sued, but this guy didn't go after the car manufacturer and didn't go after the track, he only went after me.

Now, by the end of the 1960s firesuit technology had come a long way, but it wasn't nearly as advanced as it is today. Even in our own literature we essentially told our customers that after 12 seconds of exposure to fire they were on their own. I used to say, "Up to 12 seconds we can give you some protection. After that it's up to the Man Upstairs." Our contention was that this guy had been adequately protected for those 12 seconds and that his burns came later on. The plaintiff's attorney insisted that our suit hadn't done its job. That made me furious, which, as you'll see, turned out to be not such a bad thing.

We were in a courtroom in downtown Los Angeles and I was on the witness stand. The plaintiff's attorney was beating me like a rented mule, accusing me of this, accusing me of that, and suggesting to the jury that I was being less than truthful. Finally I lost my cool. I said to that attorney, "You know, you've called me a liar every way a man can call another man a liar without actually using that word. Well, I'll tell you how we can stop all this nonsense: Let me put on an identical suit and I'll light myself on fire for 12 seconds."

I'm lucky I wasn't cited for contempt. By then I'd been around enough judges to know they don't take kindly to outbursts like that.

The plaintiff's attorney said to the jury, "Ladies and gentlemen, this is just showmanship on Mr. Simpson's part . . ."

Just then the judge interrupted him and said, "Wait a minute. I think Mr. Simpson has a pretty good idea."

It was one of the few times in my life where shooting my mouth off at an inappropriate moment actually paid off.

The judge called a recess and all the appropriate parties met in his chambers. The judge said to me, "This is rather unusual, Mr. Simpson. Are you sure you want to go through with this?"

I said, "I've got no problem with any of it."

The judge had one more reservation: He wanted to clear all of this with the local fire marshal, just to be sure it was safe. Well, the fire marshal showed up, heard what we had planned, and said, "You're going to set yourself on fire? Hey, I'd like to see that!" See, he was interested in learning more about the materials and technology we were using.

That night my attorney and dear friend Alvin Cassidy said to me, "Simpson, you're crazy! Do you realize that if you get burned, we lose? We're screwed!"

I understood why Alvin was so concerned. But he had no way to know that right from the birth of the Nomex fire suit, I had done dozens of experiments that involved lighting my arms and legs on fire. Setting myself ablaze, in fact, got to be sort of standard practice after a while. One year at Indy, when I was trying to get some of the old-line guys to see the gains we had made with our latest suit, I said, "Look, I'll just put one on and you guys can light me on fire." Well, they went for that. I sat on a metal chair while they poured gasoline on me and then George Snider threw in a match. The suit held up fine. Not only was it a great test of my commitment to building a solid product, it was also a perfect example of the hardass sense of humor we all had back then: As I sat there in the flames, through the haze I could see one of those crazy bastards—I think it was Johnny Rutherford—sticking a hot dog into the fire.

I told Alvin not to worry, that we'd be all right.

The next day they moved the trial—judge, jury, stenographer, the whole deal—into the courtyard of the Los Angeles County Court-house. We had a small amount of gasoline to get the fire started and two guys on hand with fire extinguishers, who were supposed to put me out after 15 seconds or if I signaled that I was burning up. I was asked to go to the judge's chambers, where the judge compared the plaintiff's suit with mine to ensure they were identical. Then, in the presence of the judge and the bailiff, I stripped down and got into that suit.

Next we all went outside. The judge had decided he should be the one to hold the stopwatch, so he got into position. I sat down in a chair, they poured the gasoline on me, and they threw a match in my direction. The flames came up with a whoosh. I happened to be looking straight at the judge at that moment, and he *dropped* the stopwatch. I mean, he freaked. I guess he'd never seen a man lit on fire before.

I let the thing keep burning, because nobody was sure exactly how much time had elapsed. When I finally signaled for the extin-guishers and the fire was put out, someone picked up the stopwatch. It read something like 20 or 25 seconds.

I changed my clothes in the judge's chambers—again in front of the judge and the bailiff—and went back to the witness stand. My at-torney asked if I had any burns and I said no. He asked if I would re-move my pants to prove that and I did. My legs were fine.

That was the end of the case right there. Four minutes after the closing arguments, the jury was back with a verdict in our favor.

Score another one for the good guys.

Unfortunately, court cases are a lot like everything else in life: Sometimes you win, sometimes you lose, and it isn't always fair.

I got into a bad situation in 1984. A boy had been killed while racing a motorcycle at a road course in New Hampshire. It was a tragic accident, one of those things that you obviously wish hadn't happened, but it did. This kid flew off his bike, smacked his head on the race track and then slid into an abutment and ended up dead. All of the usual parties got sued, including me, because the kid was wearing a Simpson helmet.

My thoughts on cases like this are pretty simple: If you strap on a helmet bearing a Simpson label, you're wearing a damn good helmet. But one of the facts of the racing life is that when you hit an immovable object at high speed, you might be hurt and you might even die. Sure, maybe the gods will intervene and you'll stand up, dust yourself off, and laugh about the whole thing over a beer. But you *might* be hurt and you *might* die. This kid died.

The official cause of death was a basal skull fracture. Everyone sees the words "skull fracture" and the first thing they think is that the guy's head was busted open. The fact is, a basal skull fracture involves the brain being torn from the brain stem because of the deceleration forces; when the body stops moving, the brain and the stem do not stop at the same instant and they separate. It has little to do with how well the head is protected from the outside because you can have a basal skull fracture without your head hitting a damn thing.

The case was heard in a civil court in Concord, New Hampshire, and I knew we were in trouble from the start. There were all these so-called experts arguing about helmet construction, about the properties of fiberglass, about all kinds of scientific theories. Maybe all that technical stuff went right over the heads of the jurors, I don't know. Maybe they just felt sympathy for the dead boy's family. The bottom line was, they ruled in favor of the plaintiff and their judgment against us was in the millions of dollars.

It was a numbing, catastrophic verdict for me. Don't forget, this was in a time when nobody in our industry knew much about product liability insurance, how it could protect you against lawsuits like this one. This was a direct hit against me and against everything I had tried for years to build. I was absolutely devastated, emotionally and financially.

Of course it could have been much worse. Because the industry was seeing so many lawsuits, Alvin Cassidy had advised me earlier that it would be smart to make each division of my business a separate entity; my firesuit company was separate from my helmet company, which was separate from my seat belt company and so on. This way if one division ran into difficulties, it wouldn't directly impact the others. It cost me probably an extra $100,000 a year to operate that way, but it turned out to be a smart thing to do because the New Hampshire judgment affected only the helmet-making end of the business.

Still, it was a crippling blow. I had to file bankruptcy proceedings, Chapter 11, to keep from losing every asset and every piece of equipment the helmet company owned. Naturally, as soon as that happens, word gets out that you're in trouble. Like any growing company, we had some outstanding loans; the banks, which were afraid of losing their money, immediately called them due.

There was hell to pay. It was the beginning of a very dark, painful period in my life, two years of nothing but bad times. I was on my knees. I went through a long stage where I wasn't eating, wasn't sleeping. It was a make-or-break moment for my company and I was all too aware of that.

It was then that I made one of the pivotal decisions of my life. I knew that if we were to survive, I would have to keep—or in some cases regain—the trust of the network of distributors and dealers I had spent 25 years putting together. The problem was, establishing trust is a hard thing to do through a long-distance telephone call and

I sure didn't have the wherewithal any more to fly around the country visiting them. At the time I had only two things in my life I could count on: my girlfriend Cynthia (who later became my third wife) and a BMW that I owned. When you're down, you look to your strengths. Cynthia and I packed all our clothes into that little car and set out on a cross-country mission to keep those dealers and distributors on my side.

It wasn't easy, not for a minute. You've heard the old saying about the guy who didn't own a pot to piss in or a window to toss it out of? That was pretty much me, once that lawsuit was finished, so this was the ultimate low-budget trip. We stowed our Hibachi in the trunk of the car and every night our meals consisted of grilled vegetables we bought at whatever roadside stands we came across. It was a healthy way to eat, I guess, but it didn't make me feel very good. I was a guy who was just starting to get used to the finer things in life, good food and good restaurants; now here I was, loading up our little grill with charcoal and cooking up a three-dollar dinner for two by the side of the highway, just trying to survive.

As tough as it was, that trip paid off. It showed our dealers and distributors that I might have been down, but I wasn't out. Most of them had the faith to stick with us, and if I was a betting man I'd wager that those personal visits had a lot to do with that.

In the end we dissolved the helmet end of the business, but that turned out to be just a temporary thing, thanks in large part to another fellow who apparently had a lot of faith in me: my old pal Parnelli Jones.

When we auctioned off the assets of the helmet company, Parnelli purchased all the tooling, which was the most important part of the business. That sort of puzzled me, because although Parnelli had a lot of racing-related business interests, building helmets wasn't one of them. I found out soon enough what he was up to. When things stabilized for us, Parnelli sold all that equipment right back to me. He had only bought it to make sure I wasn't left high and dry if I ever chose to get back in the helmet game, which I did in 1988.

*Parnelli Jones: Look, Bill was a friend of mine, and you help your friends. I didn't think too much about it; I just saw that he needed moral support, support from his friends, so I gave him some.*

There were a few other folks who, like Parnelli, helped me weather that storm. Two of them, Jim Williams of Golden State Foods and George Middleton of Pizza Hut, were wealthy businessmen, giants in their fields. I had met Jim and George through racing and we had become friendly. How friendly? Well, both of those guys offered me any amount I needed—I mean, unlimited money—to get us through our lowest days after the New Hampshire lawsuit.

*Jim Williams, longtime friend: Let me tell you a little something about the uniqueness that first attracted me to Bill Simpson. He is a guy who literally has two voices. One is the voice he uses at the race track, or when he's out partying. I enjoy Bill's humor and I get a kick out of that voice. But when you sit and talk with him about safety, his voice actually changes. The sincerity comes out, the way it does in anybody who has a real passion for something.*

*So I have two friends in Bill Simpson. One is the guy I have a good time with and the other is the guy who has a passion and concern for the safety end of this sport. And I think it's that passion and concern that cements our ongoing relationship. My offer to help him was made just because I admired that side of him so much. It was unconditional help, anything he needed.*

Ultimately I declined those offers, because I figured it was my problem to get out of, not theirs. But I'll never forget their generosity. And there were other people who helped in different, more subtle ways. On that ride across America we made a pretty long pit stop in Indianapolis. Having spent so many months of May there, I had come to look at the city as kind of a second home and I had made a lot of friends there. I hung out with some of those folks on that extended stay, and the way they helped me keep my chin up was appreciated more than they will ever know.

> **Wayne Leary:** *At the time Simpson was pretty down. He had put up with one lawsuit after another, and that one [in New Hampshire] knocked the shit out of him. I had gotten out of racing, but I had a hot-rod shop in Indianapolis. When he was in town he would come by with that little Hibachi and we'd cook up some corn and drink a few beers, and we just got closer and closer.*
>
> *And you know something? I've still got that Hibachi. The guy who finally ended up buying Simpson's BMW figured it went along with the car, but I told him he couldn't have it. Right now it's sitting on a shelf at my shop.*

Later on, once I bought all my tooling back from Parnelli and started gearing up to build helmets again, I based that end of our operation right there in Indianapolis. Maybe it was a way for me to be sure I'd keep in touch with the friends who had not let me down when things got rocky.

Of course there were others who tried to stomp me into the ground during that same stretch. My competition, especially Bell, did their best to bury me, but I understood that. Hell, we were in the same business, and any company in Bell's position would have tried to capitalize on my misfortune. What I couldn't rationalize was the way I was abandoned by some of the folks I had previously done business with, like certain suppliers who cut us no slack at all in our Chapter 11 hearings. We had always enjoyed what I thought were great relationships, but now they treated me as if we were complete strangers. When I got back on my feet I dealt with those people the only way I knew how: I vowed to never again do business with any of them. I haven't and I won't, strictly out of principle.

See, this ol' elephant has a long memory.

I guess I see myself as a fairly principled guy. I am very big on honesty and I have what I feel is a strong sense of right and wrong.

Way back when, I found out that one of my employees, a guy I had really trusted, was selling some helmets on the side and keeping the money. There was no question about it. I had an investigation done and we had the goods on him. Well, I wanted to teach my sons a lesson about honesty and here was my chance. I brought them into my office, sat them on the sofa and said, "Boys, I want you to see what happens when people have no respect for honesty." And I called this fellow in.

I told him I was aware of the stealing and that there was no use arguing about it. He wanted to argue anyway. Well, the argument ended when I went over the desk and whipped his ass. Then I dragged him outside and threw him off my property. That probably wasn't the smoothest way for a parent to act in front of his children, but I know this: The lesson hit home with my sons. They learned about honesty and about the consequences of not being honest.

I said, "Boys, remember this: Your integrity is the only thing you leave as a legacy." I believe that, and I always have.

If you stick to the truth, or at least to what you believe to be true, things will almost always work out in the end. I feel very strongly that when you discuss something with somebody, you need to tell them what you really think, not what you're guessing they want to hear. I suppose that makes me a bit different, because I've met a lot of people who would rather climb a tree to tell a lie than stand on the ground and tell the truth. But that's the way I am.

Now, there were times when I could have said what I was thinking in slightly quieter tones. I certainly have been a little too vocal on occasion, I can see that. Over the years I made some enemies—among my fellow racers, among sanctioning body officials, even within the safety industry—because I was never afraid to call a spade a spade.

    *Bill Vukovich Jr.: When my son Billy went from Super-modifieds to Indy cars, I ran into Simpson at Billy's first race, which was at Phoenix [in 1988]. Simpson and I had been friends for years, of course, and he said, "Hey, why don't you work for me at Indy during the month of May?" I did that and later on I worked for him full-time, going to all kinds of race tracks.*

    *Well, the next February we went to Daytona. As soon as we got there, Elmo Langley, who used to drive the pace car, came over and said that [NASCAR vice-president] Les Richter wanted to see me. Simpson said, "What do you suppose he wants?" I told him it was probably just a social thing. I'd known Les for years; we're both from Fresno, both in the Fresno Racing Hall of Fame. So I found Les and we talked for a minute. Then he said, "Vuky, I've got to tell you something about your boss. I don't know how he acts when he's at the Indy car races, but we do not like his attitude around here." I said, "Well, why don't you just tell him that yourself?" And Les said, "Because I'm afraid that if I confront him, he'll blow up at me. Then I'll have to run his ass out of here, which I don't want to do. If you tell him, he'll have time to cool off before he sees me."*

    *I went back and saw Simpson, and he asked me what Richter had said. I told him, "Oh, it's the same old shit. They think you're an asshole."*

In those days that's just the way I was. If I felt something was amiss, I didn't have any problem telling people about it, and there were times when a lot of important people in motor racing would have preferred I didn't do that. Hell, for a couple of years I wasn't exactly welcome at the National Hot Rod Association's major drag races because I had shot my mouth off about things I thought needed to be corrected. This falling out with the NHRA meant I didn't get to see a lot of my old drag-racing buddies as often as I wanted to, but that was a price I was willing to pay. Every time I opened my mouth I was doing what my conscience told me to do.

> **Don Prudhomme:** *For a while there, Simpson disagreed with NHRA on every goddam thing they did. A lot of guys felt the same way he did, but he was one of the few who would stand up and say so.*

> **Dick Berggren:** *Simpson has always been unafraid to speak out when he saw something wrong. Even now, no one has the courage he has when it comes to that sort of thing.*

I still shoot my mouth off, but I don't seem to get in nearly the amount of hot water I once did. I think there's a couple of reasons for that: Number one, I hope I've learned over the years to be a little bit more diplomatic when I'm dealing with sensitive issues. And number two, I'd like to believe that people have come to see me as a guy who is genuinely concerned about this stuff, and as a guy who has spent a lot of sleepless nights building up a track record in the field of safety, rather than as just some rabble-rouser.

> **Roger Penske:** *The guy might like to raise hell, but at the end of the day he's got a lot that he stands for. He's done a lot for this sport and he's stayed in it. A lot of guys in the racing business have come and gone, but Simpson was there early on and he's still there.*

In fact in the last 15 years this old rabble-rouser has somehow become—are you ready for this?—an accepted member of the motorsports establishment. I'm humbled to point out that, since the mid-'80s, several organizations have seen fit to honor me and my company with various awards and distinctions: the Indianapolis Motor Speedway's Continental Casualty Award of Excellence in 1985; the United States Air Force Executive Performance Award in 1987;

the CART Carl Horton Humanitarian Award in 1988; the *Car Craft* Magazine Person of the Year Award, 1989; the NCRA Award for Outstanding Dedication, the NHRA Award for Active Involvement and Support, the Indy 500's Switzer Award of Excellence (which I shared with Luciano Aguirre) and the United States Air Force Executive Commander Performance Award, all in 1990; the *Car Craft* Magazine Manufacturer of the Year Award in 1991 and '94; the Jack O'Neal Award in 1992; and a Boy Scouts citation for "outstanding leadership in helping build a better American community" in 1996.

They've also seen fit to vote me into the SEMA Hall of Fame (1989), the International Motorsports Hall of Fame (1998) and the Living Legends of Auto Racing Hall of Fame (2000).

> ***Johnny Rutherford:*** *If there was ever a single humanitarian award for all of motorsports, Bill Simpson would certainly be one of the recipients.*

> ***Jim Williams:*** *Whatever awards he has gotten—and he's gotten quite a few—aren't enough. He should get a hell of a lot more.*

I get asked a lot about being honored in this way and my natural reaction is to try to make it look like it's no big deal. I guess I'm just used to being a hardass. But if you want the truth, that stuff means more to me than I have ever let on. When your peers in the industry recognize your work, that's as high a compliment as you can receive. Every single time it happens I'm unbelievably impressed and unbelievably proud.

And not just proud of myself. I'm proud of everyone who has contributed to the growth of Simpson Race Products, whether they're still with the company or not. I know this: I may be the guy who gets to stand up at these ceremonies and hold the plaques, but they aren't mine alone. They truly belong to the people who have been by my side, from the R&D people to the workers at our plants to the men and women who have represented us at the race tracks.

There's no mistake about that; every step of the way I have been accompanied by the best people there are. Without them I'd just be a guy who had a lot of ideas.

Those people, and the things they have helped me do, have made the good times better and made the bad times, even the worst times, just distant memories.

# 9

# Making Up for Lost Time

When you get to a certain point in life, you notice more and more people asking you if you have any regrets. It's their way of letting you know that you're getting old, I guess. And I suppose the answer is just like Sinatra sings it in that song: "Regrets? I've had a few. . . ."

One is that between all the crazy circumstances that were thrust upon me as a boy and the fact that I started this business so young, I gave up most of my youth. The hours I sank into racing and working made it impossible to just be a kid, which is what I probably should have done a while longer.

Another big regret is that I never spent enough time with my sons. I mean, I love Jeff and David and I always have, but I'm sure there were plenty of times when they didn't believe that. When they were just little boys I was always off racing and looking after the business. By the time they were grown up, I was long gone.

I married their mother—my first wife, Janice—when I was just 19. Looking back on it, I can say flat out that I was too young and too immature to walk down the aisle, and it was certainly a mistake for us to do that. We only stayed married for about five years before, inevitably, it ended in divorce. But if the marriage was a failure, my life was better for it because it produced my sons.

Still, my divorce from Janice was a sign of things to come. From that point on, all my relationships with women, whether wives or girlfriends, have come to miserable conclusions. That's just the way things have gone for me. The personal side of my life has been a total failure. An absolute, complete and total failure.

My second marriage, to Christina, was an adventure right from the day those Argentine pistoleros escorted us downtown to pick up our marriage license. I don't know what the success rate is for shotgun weddings, but I'm 0-for-1 in the handgun-wedding category. The union of Bill and Christina Simpson lasted just three years before we were divorced, in 1978. Sadly, she passed away recently, in November of 1998, from lymphoid cancer.

The third time is supposed to be the charm, or so I'm told, but I'm not sure that applies to matrimony. I lived with my third wife, an artist named Cynthia Engelstad, for about 12 years before we decided it was time to get married. We passed a lot of that time at the ranch I owned up in Jackson, Wyoming, and those were a dozen chaotic years. Cynthia was with me through my roughest days, in the '80s, and she was there when I got things turned around for the better and both the company and I rebounded. We were engaged when I built my home on Lake Norman, in North Carolina, and moving into that house seemed to signal the start of a settling-down period. We were married a short time later. Unfortunately, we were apparently a whole lot better at being housemates than we were at being husband and wife, because just over a year later we were separated and on the way to my third visit to divorce court.

This would be a pretty poor romantic history if it stopped right there, but it doesn't. I've had other relationships end disastrously. Every one of them fell apart, I'm sad to say, because of me. Frankly, I don't know how the hell some of these women stood me as long as they did.

My trouble is that my best professional attribute is also my biggest personal problem: I'm driven, to the point where I'm almost single-minded. That single-mindedness can serve a guy well when he's trying to grow a business, but it's not the greatest trait to bring to a romance. When you're sitting with your lady on a quiet night in front of the fireplace, it's not a good thing when she's thinking about your relationship and you're thinking about something a million miles away. In my case that something happened to be racing safety.

Safety was never something I could think about for eight hours a day and then forget about at night. It was always a 24-hour-a-day, seven-day-a-week deal. I could push it to the background, but I could never completely switch it off. That kind of dedication takes a hell of a lot out of a person and, sadly, what's left over isn't always enough to sustain a marriage or a solid relationship. I'm not trying to make excuses. I'm just facing the facts: I never devoted the right amount of time or attention to keeping the home fires burning.

Even before the business got as big as it has, I wasn't always the easiest person to be with anyway. Maybe that stemmed from growing up the way I did, I don't know; all I know is that I was already something of a hard person and the pressure of the business certainly made me harder still. I am very much aware that there are times when I can be tough to get along with, and that goes for friends as well as lovers.

It's a process that just sort of happened. When you have to mold yourself into a boss at a young age, and over time you have 500 people working under you, maybe it's inevitable that you end up talking to everybody as if they're employees.

> **David Lawson:** *With Simpson nobody is ever exempt from an ass-chewing. Because of that, everybody is scared of him. He's got what I call his Three-Minute Rule and his Three-Second Rule. The Three-Minute Rule is that when he's in one of his moods, every three minutes he's bugging you about something new. And the Three-Second Rule is, if you don't respond within three seconds of him bugging you, he starts screaming.*

My personality—meaning, I guess, my temper—has cost me dearly at times. I've lost or came damn close to losing a pretty wide assortment of friends, girlfriends and employees over one blow-up or another, some of them over silly little things.

*Bill Vukovich Jr.: Was Simpson a tough guy to work for? Sure he was. I mean, he got on my ass every day about something. But let me tell you how I handled that: One day up at Michigan he was hollering about this or that and I said, "Bill, I know how to fix this. There's my company van. I'll find myself a ride home. I quit." And I just started walking away. Well, Simpson came running up behind me, saying, "Hey, Vuky, why don't we talk this out like gentlemen?" I ended up staying, but we had to have that conversation a few more times.*

*Jim Williams: I've always said that anybody who's employed by Simpson and carries a lunch to work is one optimistic sonofabitch.*

*Mary Walker, secretary, Simpson Race Products: I had one of Bill's old drag-racing friends call a while ago and when he heard my voice he said, 'Hey, you're still there! You must be deaf or have very thick skin.' I told him it was probably a little bit of both.*

*It took me a while, maybe a year or more, to learn that when Bill got angry he wasn't necessarily attacking me. He's just venting, and if you're the closest target you're going to hear it.*

*Denise Belle Isle, assistant secretary, Simpson Race Products: It really is like Mary says: If Bill happens to direct one of those displays at you, you just have to keep in mind that it's probably not about you. He's not the kind of guy who says things just to hurt your feelings. In fact he's really a compassionate person, although I don't think a lot of people see that side of Bill Simpson. They see his exterior, but they don't get close enough to see the other side of him.*

*I enjoy Bill's vigor. I find it amusing, in a way. He will say things that other people just wouldn't dream of saying be-*

*cause he's right up front with everything. I like that boldness,
that honesty. So I look at his displays of temper with a little
bit of humor.*

It's too late to go back and mend a lot of the fences I've knocked
over, and that bothers me. But those friendships I have managed to
sustain, I truly cherish. My closest friends, guys like Wayne Leary,
seem to understand me. I guess the best way to say it is that they accept me, or at least put up with me, despite my faults.

*Wayne Leary: The trick with Simpson is to figure out
what kind of mood he's in and go from there. When I know
he's in a shitty mood I just avoid him. I suddenly come up
with something else to do.*

Leary has been my pal forever, all the way back to the days when
he was the chief mechanic on the Indy cars Dan Gurney owned and
drove in the late '60s. Later on, in the early '70s, Dan stopped driving Indy cars and stuck Bobby Unser in the seat, and those three
guys—Gurney, Bobby and Wayne—made a habit of kicking everybody's ass. They won the USAC championship in 1974 and the Indianapolis 500 in '75, and to this day Leary is a highly respected guy
in the sport. I have always appreciated what he could do with a
wrench, but, more than that, I just plain like the guy.

Wayne and I are different kinds of people; he's as laid -back as I
am intense. But we get along, maybe because our senses of humor
seem to mesh pretty well. Sometimes I think our whole friendship is
based on the fact that we enjoy busting each other's chops.

*Wayne Leary: One year at the Speedway, when I was
just getting to know Simpson, he needed a brake rotor. Well,
Gurney's team was the dealer for Hurst-Airhart brakes. Back
then the rotors we used at Indy were the same as the ones
they ran on Top Fuel drag cars. Our list price was $75 and*

*Simpson insisted that he only paid $38 for the rotors he ran on his dragster. Naturally, I had to be a smart-ass and point out that if he looked around, he'd see that we weren't racing dragsters, we were racing Indy cars. And $75, I told him, was the going rate for an Indy car brake rotor.*

To this day, I get together with Wayne just about every time I travel to Indianapolis. We'll meet up at Kelly's Pub Too, a racing bar owned by our friend John Sears, and we'll have a few drinks and solve the problems of the world.

Of course every now and again someone will sit down with us and start talking about the old days and the stories will start flowing. That usually makes for a long night because there is no shortage of Wayne Leary stories.

Like me, Wayne once made an interesting wager with Roger Penske. In 1972, when 200 miles per hour was still a magic number in Indy car racing, Roger doubted that Bobby Unser could qualify that fast at Ontario. Leary thought different and bet Penske $500. Well, not only did Bobby qualify at over 200, but so did Jerry Grant, in Gurney's back-up car. Unser, who got a kick out of the way Leary loved to aggravate big guys like Roger, said later, "Leary knew damn good and well how fast I could go. It was like stealing from Penske."

It seems like there's a funny ending to every story Leary tells and to every story his friends tell about him. He always brings up something that happened at that Indy car race in Argentina in '71.

***Wayne Leary:*** *The pre-race meeting for drivers and chief mechanics was held in an open field. Simpson was standing right beside me and for some reason he took a step back. When he did, he fell straight down into a deep hole that had been covered over by weeds. It looked like a foxhole, but it might have been just a spot where they dug out an old tree or something. We had a pretty good laugh over that one.*

Looking up from that hole, I could see Wayne glancing around, as if to say, "Hey, where the hell did Simpson go?" I said, "Yo, man, I'm down here!" Leary pulled me out of that hole and it seems like we've been pulling each other out of one hole or another ever since.

I really enjoy Wayne's company. He is one of those people who always helps me get my mind off whatever hassles I happen to be facing at the time: racing hassles, business hassles, financial hassles, female hassles. It's important to have friends like that, because — and this may sound funny from me, as much trouble as my focus has gotten me into — they remind you that you've got to leave room in your life for the things that are really important: laughter, friendship, fun.

Maybe Bill Yeager had the best outlook on that. Nobody who watches racing from the grandstands or on television has any idea who Yeager is, but he's been around Indy cars forever. Back in the days before everybody in the sport got self-important and had to have titles on their business cards, Yeager functioned as sort of an unofficial team manager. He helped run the show at Vel's/Parnelli Jones Racing in the '70s, when Parnelli's team was as good as it got. Yeager really had his act together. To this day I'd rank him on a par with any team manager I've ever met.

Anyway, one year Yeager was in John Mecom's suite on race day at Indianapolis, and he died. That's the truth. The man had a heart attack and he died. The paramedics rushed up there and went to work on Yeager, and they hauled him off to Methodist Hospital, but everybody in the joint knew Yeager was dead. That is, everybody but Yeager. The doctors managed to revive him and Yeager pulled through. That whole episode made him an even more colorful figure around the Speedway and around the sport. These days he hangs out with the Newman-Haas team at the CART races, and he's just a guy I always love to run into.

One day Yeager and I were talking about his brush with death and it was a pretty serious, heady conversation. I said, "Tell me something, Yeager. Do you remember seeing any of those bright lights or tunnels people always talk about?"

And Yeager said, "Fuck, no. All I remember is thinking that I had too much money left in my checking account."

I've kept that in mind ever since. Not in a literal sense, because Yeager didn't mean it in a literal sense. Besides, I'm very conscious about maintaining my money at this stage of my life, probably because I'm afraid that if my business ever went into the toilet, like it has before, I wouldn't have the energy to work 16 hours a day again to build it back up.

What Yeager was saying was, when it's all said and done it's better to leave behind a pile of good times than just a pile of money.

I always had plenty of good times, but when I was young I spent too much time worrying myself to death over my business to let those good times last. I found tons of fun on the weekends without ever really looking for it, but on Monday morning I was back in the office and the laughter stopped.

Once I got solidly on my feet I tried to make up for that. I looked for fun at every opportunity and I found plenty of it.

> **Robin Miller:** When Simpson opened his [hospitality] room at the Speedway, in the early '80s, that was the place to hang out at Indy. But it was because of that room that Simpson and I almost got thrown out of the Speedway forever.
>
> Back in 1984, I think it was, I get this call from a guy at Cheri magazine. He says, "I understand you can help me get into Gasoline Alley." I say, "What do you want to do?" He says, "Well, I've got some girls who are willing to take their clothes off for a photo spread with some race cars and race drivers." So I help the guy get in.
>
> The first place we go is Kevin Cogan's garage. He's driving for Gurney. The girls start taking off their clothes and Cogan's like, "Oh, God, I'll lose my sponsor. You can't do

*this." We go over to Gary Bettenhausen's garage and Gary is
more than willing to accommodate us. So we do our little
photo shoot there. Then we go parading down to the Simpson
room, where the girls proceed to take off all their clothes.
They've got Simpson decals plastered over their private
parts. It's just out of control.*

*I remember one driver's wife or girlfriend being in there,
and she was completely appalled. But not as appalled as
Parnelli Jones was. Parnelli had showed up at the beginning
of May, walked into the Simpson room and just never left; I
mean, he had been in that room all month. Well, this one day
he decided to take, like, a 20-minute break to walk around,
and while he was gone this naked show took place. Parnelli
couldn't believe what he missed.*

*When these shots came out in the magazine, somebody
sent it to Charlie Thompson, the late superintendent of the
Speedway, and now Simpson and I were in trouble. They
wanted to know how all of this had happened and Simpson
just said, "Honest, I have no idea."*

*Man, he was a fun guy to be around.*

A lot of our fun was a little bit off-color, for sure. With us racing
wasn't necessarily a family sport, if you happened to be on the loud
side of the pit fence. But there were also a lot of times when we just
had good, clean fun, playing practical jokes or hanging out with the
kinds of friends who were always ready for a laugh.

***Linda Conti, former Simpson employee:** Simpson can
be kind of devilish. The more fun he can have getting things
stirred up, the more he'll plot and plot and plot. If he thinks
he can get five minutes of fun out of something, he'll do
whatever it takes. The Ayrton Senna story is a great example.*

*In the early '90s I worked for Bill, primarily in open-
wheel racing. I spent most of my time concentrating on*

*Formula One and the CART series, and of course I'd spend the month of May at Indianapolis. In Formula One I worked closely with Team Lotus because their drivers wore Simpson gear, and I was also trying to recruit some of the other F1 drivers. We'd look at guys who were wearing brands other than Simpson and if we thought we might be able to get them to use our products we'd have a helmet made and painted for them, just so they could look at it. For example, we had an Ayrton Senna helmet made up; I had actually met with Senna and talked with him about maybe switching over [from a rival brand].*

*It just so happened that in 1993 a bunch of new helmets had come back from the painter in the first week of May, and because we were all out at the Speedway we installed the helmet liners and interiors right there in the [hospitality] room. We had helmets for all the Indy car guys, but there was also a Mika Hakkinen helmet lying around, because Hakkinen was a Lotus driver, and there was this Ayrton Senna helmet too.*

*Well, that was the year people had been talking about Senna maybe racing Indy cars, and he had even tested one of Penske's cars out at [Firebird Raceway in] Phoenix over the winter. So a few of us were hanging around and some-body said, "You know what would be kind of fun? Let's start a rumor that Senna is here and he's going to run the 500 for Penske!"*

*Simpson might not have had the original idea, but he egged it on. He had [longtime Simpson rep] Ray Briskey take the helmet over to the Speedway's medical office to get it certified. That really got people buzzing. Then Jim Williams, who was one of Penske's sponsors and got a kick out of all this, said, "Hey, Linda, can we get a suit made up to go with the helmet?" I told him it could be done overnight. So Jim or-dered a blue suit and we had 'Ayrton Senna' stitched on the* belt and big Marlboro patches on the front and back. When the suit came, we left it lying around so people would see it. Then whenever someone walked in, we'd act surprised: "Oh, quick, hide that suit!" Before long, this rumor was everywhere.

Well, we decided to take things a step further. Mike King —who is now one of the radio voices of the 500, but was working for a TV station out of Terre Haute back then— happened to be about the same size as Senna. Mike did live broadcasts every day at noon and six o'clock, but he had a lot of free time in between. I clued him in on what we had done and I said, "How would you like to be Ayrton Senna for an afternoon?"

Mike got dressed in the bathroom of the Simpson room. Once he put on the helmet and gloves, you had no idea it wasn't Senna. Meanwhile we had lured a few press guys over, supposedly to talk about something else, and they caught a glimpse of Mike. Then we had somebody come over with one of Team Penske's golf carts. Mike came out, jumped on the cart, and was driven over to the Marlboro hospitality tent. He disappeared into the tent, and before long there were writers, photographers and TV cameras swarming outside.

The whole thing worked perfectly. In fact, we found out later that in Japan the TV stations interrupted their regular programming to run a bulletin about Ayrton Senna racing at Indianapolis.

It all came to a screeching halt when the phone rang in the Simpson room. I picked it up, and [Speedway president] Tony George was on the other end. He said, "Is there something going on at my race track that I ought to know about?" I thought to myself, If I ever want a [500 credential] badge again, I'd better 'fess up. I told him that Simpson and Jim Williams had a little too much free time on their hands. Tony just laughed and said, "OK, thanks."

*Jim Williams: One night back in the early '90s at Indy, a bunch of us decided to go for a motorcycle ride. We ended up in some town about 50 miles outside Indianapolis. We pulled up in front of a little bar and we parked our motorcycles. Well, when Bill climbed off, he forgot to put down his kickstand. It was like a domino effect—all the bikes went down. Then we all went into the place and the first thing we realized was that these folks did not like motorcycle people. That was clear. But the first one of us to pull off his helmet was Roger Penske, the next guy to take his off was Rick Mears, and then Danny Sullivan and then Simpson and so on. Naturally the folks in the bar recognized everybody. Let me tell you, for a place that didn't like motorcycle people, they treated us pretty good. In fact they weren't serving food that night, but they ended up making us dinner.*

We had fun in every race town we went to, and sometimes we had fun at places that seemed a million miles away from joints like Indianapolis. Hell, I even figured out ways to have fun when I was supposed to be home doing nothing.

*Parnelli Jones: My wife and I were guests at Bill's ranch in Wyoming, and one day we heard about this little fairgrounds about 30 miles down the road that was having a demolition derby in a couple days. I didn't think much about it until I woke up in the middle of the night and heard all this noise:* bang, crash, bang! *I went outside, and there's Simpson, knocking the windows out of the car he had been driving on the street. It was a pretty nice car, but he had somehow decided he wanted to run it in that demolition derby.*

*On the day of the event he sent somebody to the fairgrounds with that car while we climbed into his jet and flew over there. It was only 30 miles, like I said, but he didn't want to drive, so we flew. Those people thought we were nuts, flying a jet in for a demolition derby.*

My basic strategy was this: I worked hard and I played hard. If things got out of hand occasionally, that might have been because I did a lot of my playing in saloons. That's not an excuse; I did some stupid things, and the booze didn't make them any less stupid. But at least it allowed me to plead temporary insanity from time to time.

**David Lawson:** *Simpson spent a long time in what I call his Really Big Screw-Up Era.*

**John Nicotra, longtime friend:** *One night I met up with Bill and Cynthia at a club in Fort Lauderdale. There was a band playing and the place was packed. Everybody was out on the dance floor, having a good time. Eventually the party died down and the only two people left in the place, the last of the Mohicans, were me and Simpson. Both of us had been drinking pretty good. Well, Simpson struck up a conversation with the bandleader. He said, "You know, I'm pretty friendly with Henry Mancini." The bandleader picked right up on that; he listened very intently, wanting to know all about Henry Mancini. So Simpson said, "Henry once told me this: the louder a band is, the less talented they are. And you know something? Y'all are about the loudest sonsabitches I have ever heard."*

**Tom McEwen:** *When Simpson would party . . . oh, man. There were nights when we'd go to a restaurant and have a few drinks after dinner and he'd end up tearing the joint down. There were a lot of places we couldn't go back to.*

**Don Prudhomme:** *I never ran with Bill as much as some guys did, but we hung together for a while. I've been through some drinking stuff with him, and some partying. He's just a tough sonofabitch. He'll fight in a heartbeat.*

**John Sears, proprietor, Kelly's Pub Too:** *In all the years I've owned Kelly's, we've only had three major fights.*

*Bill Simpson was in two of them and he started the other one.*

**Wayne Leary:** *Simpson has mellowed in some ways. But, you know, you can still light him off pretty easily. That's no problem whatsoever.*

**Jim Williams:** *Simpson was in the men's room at Kelly's and I guess some guy made a crack at him. I was having a beer with Leary and the rest of the gang, and here came Simpson and this other guy crashing through the men's room door, fighting. But it wasn't much of a fight, really; both of them were overserved and overweight, so instead of hooking and jabbing they were rolling around on the floor. It looked like something out of the WWF.*

*Another night Penske was going to meet us at Kelly's so we could all go motorcycle riding. Well, John Sears has a lot of nice racing memorabilia there and one of the things he had was a great big Lola Cars sign that had come right from the Lola factory. It was a beautiful piece, made of wood with a lot of nice inlaid artwork. Simpson saw that thing and he was thinking that Roger—who, of course, raced his own Indy cars against the Lolas—might not like having a Lola sign in the place. So he walked over there and put his foot right through the thing. I mean, Simpson just destroyed what was probably a classic piece of memorabilia. He and Sears got divorced for a while after that, but of course they eventually smoothed things over.*

I'm not proud to say it, but I've gone out of control a few times. I know that. One day I got pissed off at a guy about something, so I drove out to where he lived and crashed my truck right through the wall of his house and into the living room. And if you thought my entrance was spectacular, my exit was even better. When I put the transmission into reverse and mashed the gas to get the hell out of there, my tires dug in and threw his carpeting right up onto the wall. It was something else.

> **John Martin:** *I was taking care of his son Dave's car back in '86, when we all went over to England to run the Formula 3 series. One day we were riding down the street in London, with me driving, and I was trying to make a turn, but this guy in a Volkswagen pulled up beside me and just wouldn't let me turn. Well, that upset Bill a little bit. He said, "Just pass him." So I stood on the gas, and as we went by the guy, Bill threw open his door and, uh, put his autograph on the side of that Volkswagen about five times.*

I'll admit that my brand of behavior hasn't always suited everybody I came in contact with. Because of that there have been a few people who joined me and my friends for one mission or another and never came back to re-enlist.

But I do have a number of acquaintances who overlook my occasional outbursts and enjoy themselves enough to sign on for return engagements.

David Lawson is one of those guys. He's one of the few friends I have who isn't directly involved in motorsports, although he did a little bit of road racing and some off-road stuff before we met, almost 30 years ago. Lawson looks like an old surfer, but he's a pretty sharp cat; he's college-educated and he spent a few years in the world of big business, working for Proctor & Gamble. Today he lives out in California and he looks after some of the property I own out there. He also happens to be one of my closest friends.

> **David Lawson:** *A lot of people don't understand how we're still so friendly, because he tends to drive people away sometimes. But, you know, I love the shit out of him. I can't help it. I'd do anything for the guy and I think he'd do the same for me. If Simpson likes you, he really likes you.*

Somewhere along the line Lawson got drafted into service as my companion in a hundred different adventures, including almost all of my marine excursions. More often than not, if I'm off someplace on my boat, David is right there with me.

> **David Lawson:** *When we met, Simpson had his business going, but he hadn't really made any money at it. He had nothing, really. Later on, once he'd made a little bit of money, we started to go on these journeys. First they were small trips; we'd rent a motorhome and go down to Mexico, stuff like that. As he accumulated his wealth the trips got more elaborate. We'd jump on airplanes and boats and wind up in Central America or somewhere else. We used to have a saying: "An island a day."*

Once Lawson and I got into the boating thing, we didn't mess around. What I mean is, we always went in style. For a while I had a 52-foot boat I called *Sun Chaser*. I put about 80,000 miles on her over a 10-year period. Then I got another boat, one I christened *Dog Pound* because I always seemed to be in the dog house with various women, friends and racing organizations.

Our first big trip aboard *Dog Pound* started out simply enough. We wanted to explore the Rio Dolce—which translates to "sweet river"— in Guatemala, on the western edge of the Caribbean.

> **David Lawson:** *Guatemala was fun. We took* Dog Pound *up this big river surrounded by nothing but jungle and birds and monkeys. I mean, it was real primitive. We stopped at a marina that had a small hotel; actually, it was just some little huts built up over the water. In the morning I was brushing my teeth in my hut and I happened to look down into the sink. I could see daylight; the sink just emptied straight down into the river. There was no plumbing. Naturally the toilet was the same way. It was a pretty trippy place.*

*Christmas was coming up, so each of us went home for a few days, but we went back to Guatemala on New Year's Day. We flew into Guatemala City and from there we hired a small single-engine plane to fly us back to where the boat was. We're flying over miles and miles of jungle. I'm not really paying attention, but Simpson's looking at the instruments and he tells me that the magneto gauge is fluctuating. All I know is that means we're in trouble. Somehow we make it to this tiny airport, where there's a guy waiting for us. He's got a tractor with a little cart behind it. Simpson and I climb into this cart and the guy drives us down to the river. From there we climb into a little ponga boat and we catch a ride to the marina.*

*When we get back to the boat it turns out that the woman who owned the hotel had died the day before. Everybody in the marina is in mourning, to the point where we can't get anything to eat, can't even buy a beer. Naturally Simpson goes nuts about that, so we pull up stakes and head down the river.*

That ended up being some trip, all right. Lawson calls it "the grand adventure" and he isn't kidding. We went all over Central America—Costa Rica, Belize, Honduras, El Salvador, through the Panama Canal a few times—and saw just about everything there was to see. What started out as a simple little ride up the Rio Dolce ended up lasting for months, off and on.

In the end we kind of ran out of places to go down there, so we decided to head across the Gulf of Mexico to Key West, in Florida, and close out the grand adventure with a little bit of fishing.

**David Lawson:** *We were going to leave for Key West from Cancun, where the boat was sitting. It was supposed to be a three-day trip. We went to dinner in Cancun, got back to the boat at five o'clock and headed out. We cruised all night* *and the next morning, right about daylight, we were just off the Marina Hemingway in Cuba.*

You know what happened? We screwed up and we wandered a little too close to Cuba. Now, if you wander too close to, say, Mississippi, that's no big deal. But the Cuban government gets really nervous about strange boats drifting into their waters; they figure you might be smuggling people off or onto the island. I guess we seemed pretty suspicious, so they kind of invited us into the harbor. They delivered that invitation by way of a nice gunboat escort and lots of waving.

> **David Lawson:** *We tied up at the marina and eight or nine officials came aboard, everybody from Cuban immigration to doctors to veterinarians, in case we had any animals. And of course every one of them had to be paid. But they were incredibly courteous; they took off their shoes when they came aboard and they were very friendly. It took about three hours to get through that checking-in procedure and then they decided we were OK. They didn't have a big problem with us being there. So Simpson and I went off to have some dinner. That was the first day of several days of goofing around in Cuba.*
>
> *One morning a couple of days later I was sitting on the boat and I noticed that the boat behind ours was flying a Russian flag. There was this bald-headed guy on board, real tan. He waved me over, told me he wanted to show me his boat. I got on board and he said, "You want a drink?"*
>
> *I said, "Well, I've never shunned one."*
>
> *He said, "What would you like?"*
>
> *I said, "Whatever you're having."*
>
> *He poured me a water glass full of rum. No ice, no nothing else, just rum. So the two of us sat and drank rum and he told me his story. It turns out he was the captain of that Soviet submarine that had collided with the American sub [in*

*the Barents Sea] back when our two countries were playing war games with each other. It sounds like a bullshit story, I know, but this guy showed us the documentation to prove it. It turns out that in the years after that incident he and the captain of the American sub had become great friends; they'd been to each other's homes and their kids all knew each other. He was a fascinating guy.*

David running into that Russian skipper turned out to be a good thing, because he was the only person we met who could find us an outgoing phone line that could handle international calls. That was pretty important because Lawson and I were seriously overdue in Key West. And, to tell you the truth, we weren't in any hurry to leave Cuba yet. We needed to let our friends and families back home know where the hell we were.

But, typically, even something as harmless as this little phone call turned crazy before too long. The Russian took us to a hotel in downtown Havana and hooked us up with the switchboard operator. Because the telephone system was so primitive I knew I'd probably have only one chance to call somebody, so I dialed Mary Walker at the office back in North Carolina. It's critical to me that Mary always knows where to find me, in case something comes up.

> ***Mary Walker:*** *Everybody tells me I'm the only person who knows where Bill is and what he's doing at all times, and I guess that's true. He'll tell me where he's going to be even when no one else knows, and from there it's up to me to decide who else should find out. That's tough, because there are all kinds of people who call here.*

I said, "Mary, I can't talk long. I'm in Cuba and everything is fine. I don't want you to worry, because there's nothing wrong . . ."

She said, "What are you doing in Cuba?"

I said, "This is not the time to ask questions." Then the connection broke off and we couldn't establish another one.

Naturally Mary was concerned. Who could blame her? I'm sure that in our brief conversation I had sounded anything but reassuring. She immediately started calling around and pretty soon everybody had it figured that we must have been in some jail in Havana. By the time I got back to the office several days later, the rumors had really spread. I'll bet we had 300 phone messages asking what was going on and wanting to know if Lawson and I were ever going to make it home.

But here's the best part: While we were gone, the Winston Cup series raced at Martinsville and one of the cars carrying an on-board camera belonged to my pal Rusty Wallace. All day long, every time that camera looked out Rusty's windshield it picked up this plea scrawled on the dashboard: "Free Havana Bill." Later on, Rusty's guys presented me that piece of his dashboard and to this day I've got it in my office as a memento of my Cuban vacation.

It ended up being one more story for the memory bank—and for this book—but our trip to Cuba stands out from the rest in one respect. For most of my life the truth has always been crazier than the stories that popped up later on; this time the stories beat the reality. People talked as if Lawson and I had sailed into Havana harbor with a battleship, guns blazing, and it wasn't nearly that dramatic. It was exciting, yes, but in the end Cuba was just another nice place we got to see.

> **David Lawson:** *I know it sounds like we've got a lot of crazy stories, but that's only because Simpson puts us into these crazy predicaments. It's like he goes out and looks for trouble.*

Even when I avoided international waters I managed to bump up against authority from time to time. Back when I had *Sun Chaser*, an innocent moonlight cruise turned into a major dilemma. I had left Palm Beach one night and was running north along the Florida coast, and in the wee hours of the morning one of the two engines quit. I wasn't worried because I knew from my navigational equipment exactly where I was, so I threw down an anchor. I figured that in the morning I'd limp into a port with my one good engine. Well, shortly after sunrise I saw two distinct sights looming in the heavy morning mist: In the distance, a NASA Space Shuttle standing against its launch tower at the Kennedy Space Center; in the foreground, a small fleet of U.S. Coast Guard ships heading my way. Turns out the Shuttle was due to blast off that morning, but they had called off the launch in order to check on an unidentified boat lurking in the area. Mine.

They boarded *Sun Chaser* and did a quick check to determine that I wasn't a spy or a lunatic looking to shoot a missile at a Space Shuttle, and then they let me go on my way. And, much later than originally planned, the Shuttle was on its way too. Oops.

These days we do our sailing on my latest boat, *Tango Sierra*, a really nice 64-foot yacht with a plush stateroom, ample sleeping quarters for any guests who come along, and plenty of gear for deep-sea fishing. Generally I'm in charge of piloting the boat and Lawson is in charge of catching fish. We've found that it's best if we stick to those roles. Oh, I know a little bit about fishing and Lawson knows a little bit about boating, but if each of us looks after his own area of expertise, things go more smoothly.

> **David Lawson:** *"One night I was steering the boat so everyone else could sleep, and Simpson had given me a heading to follow. All night long the seas got rougher and rougher, and he commented on that a couple of times but he didn't decide to do anything about it. Well, by morning we were taking green water up over the top of the boat. We had sailed into a hurricane. Naturally, that became my fault, like it was my own personal hurricane. I got my daily ass-chewing and he took over after that."*

I might be the better captain, but Lawson definitely has his area covered. I'll tell you how good a fisherman David is: Seldom do we wet a line without hauling in something big. *Tango Sierra* has a fully equipped kitchen on the main deck and a grill on the flying bridge, so when we land a fish we often have it for lunch within 10 minutes.

When I'm a few miles offshore and we've got a couple of lines in the water, I'm at peace. Some people find peace by raising roses in their gardens, but I find it out on that boat. I get out on the sea and it just cleanses my mind.

Now, that's not to say that all we do is relax. I have a habit of choosing ports of call that are, shall we say, fun places to hang out. Lately I've been partial to the Pacific coast of Mexico: Puerto Vallarta, Manzanillo, Acapulco, Ixtapa, Zihuatanejo. I'll fly to Mexico, hop on that boat and put a thousand miles on it, just moving it from Point A to Point B and sight-seeing. Mexico is a pretty cool place because there are very few rules, and that appeals to me.

> **David Lawson:** *Simpson seems to crave those kinds of places. Maybe it's because the rest of his life, when he's working, is so structured. When he gets some time off he wants to be someplace where you can do whatever you want to.*

America is a great country, the greatest in the world. But if you'll pardon me for getting a little bit political, I think we've got too many rules here. In the United States there's a law for every damn thing you can think of. I guess that helps you get through life if you're a complete idiot, but I don't think the average person needs to be regulated that much.

I mean, I understand that if I stand near a cliff, I shouldn't step too close to the edge; I don't need a flashing sign to tell me that. I understand that there are hazards from time to time on highways; I don't need warning lights every 15 feet to remind me. America treats its adults as if we were all seven years old and that makes me crazy.

Mexico is more of a common-sense place, meaning that if you just watch your ass and use your head, you'll be OK. That fits my lifestyle. In fact if the day comes when I have no more to contribute to motorsports, I just might make my home there. I've thought about building a place with a big guest house and a nice bar, a place where all my friends can come down and just hang out in the sun.

That's something I've thought about for a long time: finding a piece of land in some nice warm place and creating my own little Shangri-La, where I can lie around all day with no sound in my life but the waves lapping against the sand and the ice cubes clinking in my glass. In fact, I've been scouting for the right spot on a lot of these boat trips we've taken.

> **David Lawson:** *Simpson will say from time to time that he's looking for some place to built a resort. The reality is he'll never find it because he's never completely happy with any one place. I call it his Eternal Search, because it's not really a search at all. It's just a good reason to go on these adventures.*
>
> *But you know the funny thing? We go to all these exotic places, yet we never really do any of them justice. I mean, all we ever seem to see is a marina, a gas dock, maybe the local market and the palapa bars on the beach.*

Most of our trips now last only a few days, maybe a week. Once I'm gone that long I get a little bit restless, antsy to go to work again. I guess it's because even when I'm floating around the Pacific or the Caribbean, racing is always right there in the back of my mind.

It's not a conscious process; it's just that racing has been the only thing I've ever known, the only constant in my life. So in my quiet moments on the boat, when I ought to be concentrating on margaritas and señoritas, I'll eventually end up daydreaming about some new design for a seat belt or a pair of gloves. And it seems like every time I get back home I've got a new idea.

I don't know, maybe I'm still too focused. Maybe the same single-mindedness that always seemed to stand between me and a happy, mutually fulfilling relationship is destined to forever stand between me and complete relaxation. That bothers me. Sometimes, when I close the bedroom door at night, I ask myself if this has been the right way to live.

So, yeah, I've got a few regrets. But I'm learning to live around them. Hell, what other choice do I have? I mean, if you're human you don't come with a rewind button. So all you can do is press on, man, and hope that the good you do outweighs the bad.

> **Bill Vukovich Jr.:** *In my heart I feel like Bill Simpson and I have a special bond, and I'll tell you why. When I lost my son Billy [in a 1990 sprint car crash] I felt very, very confused. And Simpson said, 'Vuky, take off as much time as you need—two months, three months, four months, whatever—with pay.' I thought that said a lot about the type of guy he really is, and that's why I feel like we have this bond. I love that man.*

I've thought about this a lot as I've gotten older, and if I had it all to do over again—weighing the positive things my company and I have brought to automobile racing versus my own personal happiness—I'm sure I'd take the same road I took the first time around. And I'd be content with that decision.

See, I know, deep down, that because of the way I have lived my life—because of the dedication I had in the early years and because of the stuff we manufactured or pioneered and the technologies we helped advance—hundreds of old race drivers are alive and well who might not be around had I led my life differently.

> **Dick Berggren:** *I guarantee you that there are an awful lot of people—thousands, probably—who are walking around whole today as a result of Bill Simpson's work.*

> **Don Prudhomme:** *If Simpson hadn't been around, maybe someone else would have eventually come along and done the same things. But Bill was there when we needed a guy like him, and I'd have to credit him with saving a lot of lives, in all forms of racing.*

That's a hell of a thing to claim, that you have had at least some responsibility for any number of lives being saved. Maybe it comes a little bit too close to sounding boastful. But in my case I know it's true. And I can live with that.

# 10

# Slow Down, Hell!

In the last few years it has been suggested to me that a lot of guys in my position—meaning guys my age, guys who are financially comfortable—would say, "Well, it's time. Time to slow the pace a bit. Time to kick back. Time to retire."

That's a valid point, I guess, because I could certainly stop working today and not worry about where my next meal is going to come from. From a dollars-and-cents point of view, I could stop going to the office, stop going to race tracks. But I'm not about to do that.

For one thing, I still wake up every day feeling full of energy. For another thing, even when the business end of my life has been a hassle the racing end has always lifted my spirits. Besides, just about every friend I have is involved in racing in some capacity, and who wants to cut himself off from his friends?

I don't know any other way to say it: This sport has given me so much that I don't want to turn my back on it just yet. Retirement is too abstract an idea for me to deal with right now.

And on those days when I need a little inspiration to keep going, all I've got to do is look at people like my old friend Jim Williams. I've already mentioned that Jim once offered to bail me out when I was in financial trouble, but there are other reasons I think highly of him. A lot of people in racing know Jim through his association with Roger Penske; the "J. Williams Cars" logo that ran for years on Roger's Indy cars tells you how close they are. But what most people don't know is that Jim was raised in the same environment I was. By that I mean that he was one more Southern California car guy who came from nothing. Along the way he got in the food business and he met up with a fellow named Ray Kroc, who started the McDonald's hamburger chain. Eventually, through dedication and sheer hard work, Jim climbed the business ladder and became the CEO of Golden State Foods, which supplied beef and other items to the McDonald's folks.

What Jim Williams became, really, was the hamburger king of the whole goddam world.

A few years ago, when he'd had enough of the day-to-day grind of running a large business, Jim stepped away from Golden State. Now he's pretty much retired and he's got all the money he's ever going to need; I mean, the guy flies around in a huge Gulfstream jet, and if you're lucky enough to catch a ride on it his flight attendant will be happy to serve you a fresh, piping-hot McDonald's quarter-pounder, prepared right there in Jim's galley.

Jim Williams could surely sit on a beach every day for the rest of his life, work on his tan and leave the rest of the world behind. But racing is in his veins and he can't get rid of it, so he travels to major-league events whenever and wherever he wants to. And in 1999 he built what I believe is his own personal monument, the Irwindale Speedway in California. It is, without question, the finest weekly short track in America.

I admire Williams and I can certainly relate to him, because at some point in 1997 it became clear to me that I needed a change too. I was tired of my own day-to-day grind. I had been running the business just shy of 40 years by then and I was feeling increasingly burned out. I didn't like that sensation; it was making me an old man, making me grumpy, making me mean inside. But I had no idea what to do about it.

Then Humpy Wheeler, who knew nothing about these feelings I was having, brought some people to see me. Humpy, of course, is the president of the Lowe's Motor Speedway, in Charlotte, and the folks he brought in were from Carousel Capital Management, an investment-banking firm based there in North Carolina. Carousel had been looking hard at racing, wanting to buy into companies they thought had a lot of potential for growth. Simpson Race Products, they said, was on their list of promising targets.

At first I didn't know what to think. I've already said that this company is like a child to me, a child I have nurtured and fed. I had gotten used to being a single parent to that child. On the other hand I had learned enough about these investment outfits to know that if you teamed up with a good one, the infusion of capital could help your company grow by leaps and bounds. That appealed to me.

I scheduled a powwow with the Carousel people and we got together at the Charlotte track, where Rusty Wallace and I co-own one of the condominiums overlooking turn one. We spent a couple of hours there, and even though it was mostly a get-acquainted type of thing, I liked what they had to say. I have never been completely at home with briefcase guys—maybe my lack of higher education intimidates me—but the Carousel folks put me at ease.

I appreciated the fact that they didn't want to just waltz in and take over my company. They wanted to buy a stake, which ended up being two-thirds, but they also wanted me to remain on board to provide input and direction. It was key that we saw eye-to-eye on that. They had no interest in a deal that didn't include me, and I had no interest in selling if it took me out of the loop altogether.

In the days after this meeting I got away from everybody, and I mean *everybody*. I looked long and hard at everything Carousel had proposed and I couldn't see any major holes in their plan, anything that was bad for me or the company I had built.

I called them and said I wanted to pursue the matter further. In other words, yes, I was interested in doing business with them and it was time to talk numbers. From there it was simply a matter of agreeing on a price and having our lawyers work out the fine print.

Not that this was a piece of cake. There were the usual delays here and postponements there, which frustrated me more than a little bit. In fact, in February of '98 I was in Cabo San Lucas with a girlfriend and the pressure of this huge deal being so close and yet so far off finally got to me. I just got tired of my attorneys calling me constantly and I flipped out.

I was sick of hearing lawyers bicker with lawyers, sick of the last-minute technicalities that kept popping up. The papers were supposed to have been signed already and still we kept running into snags. I was as mad as I have ever been, ready to call everything off. But Peter Funston, my lawyer from Beverly Hills who was our lead attorney on all of this, calmed me down. He told me to keep looking at the big picture and not bog down in the details. The details, he said, would hammer themselves out. And he was right.

On April 1, 1998, we signed the deal. Mary Walker and Denise Belle Isle were with me when we went to Carousel's office to make everything official.

> **Mary Walker:** *Right up until the end I would have bet that Bill would never go through with it. I just believed that he wasn't ready to give up control of his company. Even on that last day, when the three of us went downtown with Peter Funston, I didn't think it was going to happen. It wasn't until we were on the elevator, going to the meeting, that I started to believe it.*

> **Denise Belle Isle:** *That day Bill was like a cat in a roomful of rocking chairs. I kept believing he was going to walk out at any time.*

> **Mary Walker:** *I think the whole thing was kind of scary to him. Bill is not a suit-and-tie guy, he's a jeans-and-cowboy-boots guy, and here we were, dealing with an office full of suits.*

When the deal was done my attorneys told me, "Six months from now, you're going to look back and say that this was either the best deal of your life or the worst deal of your life." Well, I'm here to tell you it was definitely the best deal I have ever made.

It was a terrific move for the company's future because it has provided ample capital for the research and development work we need to do. I've come to the conclusion that running a business is just like running a race team: If your team has an annual budget of $1 million and you're racing in a league where the best guys have $10 million, you're going to get your ass kicked. Well, we're not in danger of getting our ass kicked any time soon.

It was also a terrific deal for me personally, because all the things that had contributed to my burn-out—basically, the daily red tape involved in any sizable business—were no longer a part of my routine. One of Carousel's first moves was to install professional management folks, who I call our "C-guys"; you know, the CEO, the COO, the CFO. Those are the guys who now face the daily pressures I used to face. I'm still the chairman, but now I function as a chairman without having to fill a bunch of other management roles too.

I don't deal with lawyers. I don't deal with accountants. I don't deal with insurance people. Now, understand, I like the folks who do those jobs for us, I just don't like seeing them too often. When you own a business it's almost never good news when your attorneys or your bean-counters or your insurance people want to talk to you.

And I don't have to worry about meeting the payroll anymore either. Believe me, no matter how big your company is, when you're the lone guy at the top, you worry about where the money is coming from if you're paying out hundreds of thousands of dollars a week.

As a result of all this my personal schedule has changed a bunch. Today I have nothing that resembles a standard regimen. I don't have to be at the factories in Texas or California, or at the office in North Carolina, every time there's some little problem that needs to be resolved. I devote a portion of my time to the company and a portion to other interests I have, and the rest to daydreaming about ideas that always seem to relate back to the business.

What I have, at last, is a greater degree of freedom—freedom to hang out with my pals more than I used to, freedom to attend more races than I once could. That allows me to represent the company in something of a public-relations role, which is good for Simpson Race Products.

I guess you could say my basic job with the company is to serve as a figurehead, as the identifiable guy out front, and to see that the product line reflects the state of the art in safety equipment. I enjoy the first part of that—I'd be lying if I said it wasn't an ego boost to open up *USA Today* in the spring of 1999 and find a quarter-page article about me and my company—but I truly treasure the second part because it takes me back to 1958. What I mean is, I get the same thrill from tinkering with new ideas today that I got from designing our very first drag parachute back then. That sort of thing really energizes me.

Safety equipment is a challenging field because virtually everything we do is a custom job, yet the end result has to be affordable for the racer you're trying to serve. That's not easy. Hell, a good fire suit is a work of art on par with those fancy leather jackets you see some star drivers wearing, the multi-colored ones with the sponsor logos on them. But those jackets can run $1,200 and up, and the average price for one of our suits, with all its trick embroidery and all the hands-on work required, is between $700 and $800. That's amazing when you stop and consider that some of the material in a fire suit sells for $30 per square foot. And, as new technologies develop, raw materials aren't likely to get any cheaper.

Every couple of weeks I'll spend a day or two in our Texas plant, where most of our R&D people are based, and they'll just blow me away. I have at my fingertips a staff of people who are as good as it gets when it comes to executing ideas, moving them along from the daydream stage to the drawing-board stage to the production stage. I can hand these guys an idea I've sketched on a bar napkin and a few days later they'll call and say, "OK, we've lined up a couple of different sources for the material we'll need. Which way do you want to go?" Two weeks later I'll go to Texas and see a rough prototype.

They've actually been telling me to slow down a little. They say

I've been giving them too many things to do, that I'm coming up with too many ideas. I like hearing that. It makes me feel good.

I guess I've always ridden my R&D people pretty hard. When Neil Bonnett broke his sternum in a Winston Cup wreck years ago, that seemed like an injury that might be a coming trend in head-on stock car crashes. I got my troops together and said, "We have *got* to have an answer for this." My people responded; within a couple of days we had a new sternum strap that supplemented a driver's existing harness system. And, yes, we were the first to have one. For me that was a double victory: My customers were a bit safer and we beat our competition. Again.

I'm as serious as I ever was about keeping this company a step ahead of the rest. On that front my attitude didn't change just because my role in the corporate structure did. I'm still dead-ass serious about whipping the opposition's asses every chance I get. To me it's war, and it always has been.

> **A.J. Foyt:** *One time at Indy I was mad at Simpson, so I went and got another brand of helmet. Then, just to piss him off, I sent one of my guys over with the helmet to have him look at it. He threw it down and kicked it across Gasoline Alley. In fact he kicked it so hard he broke his toe.*

I'm aware that not everyone in our organization is as passionate about this sort of thing as I am, and I understand that. It's still my name on the company, so I look at it as a life-and-death struggle, whereas the average guy who works in a Simpson factory can't possibly be expected to have the same intensity. At the end of the work day those guys go home and leave their jobs behind until tomorrow. I go home too, but I just can't stop thinking about how we're going to defeat our enemies.

Unfortunately for those enemies, we're spending more time, effort and money than ever on research and development. We're always thinking about how to stay one step ahead, from the bottom of the product line to the very top.

*Bill Vukovich Jr.: This man Simpson is very close to being a genius. I mean, look at the products he's come out with, the ideas he's had. Bill's mind is going a million miles an hour all the time. This man is bright. As goofy as he is sometimes, he is very, very bright.*

In most areas we haven't had a problem staying that one step ahead. Take fibers, for instance: Every time we advance the yardstick in that particular area, it takes the copycat companies a couple years to figure out and reproduce exactly what we have done. Well, by that point we're unveiling some new fiber technology that pushes the yardstick ahead again.

Our product line for the year 2000 included a driving shoe with a trick sole made of a material that actually takes heat away from the driver's feet. I have no doubt that some of our rivals will end up copying this sole, but it'll take them a couple of years to get it right. By then we'll have something else on the shelves.

Product development is one thing I have never let up on, even when I was driving. In fact my own driving is what led to most of the ideas I had back then, because only a driver can properly tell you, in a practical way, how some of these things will or won't work.

To this day I rely on race drivers every bit as much as I rely on engineers and R&D people. I thrive on their feedback. I'm not in the cockpit anymore, so I need to hear certain things straight from a driver. I don't always know *exactly* what he's going through, because cars and speeds and tracks have changed in the last 20 years; but usually I can listen to a driver and relate to his description of things.

*Steve Krisiloff: Bill gets right in there and works with the drivers. He's always done that, and because he was involved in driving himself, he knew right away what they wanted. He couldn't always design and build the thing, but he could convey to the people working for him exactly what was needed.*

> **Rick Mears:** *A lot of times Bill didn't even have to wait for our input. By the time us drivers would sense a problem we were having, he was already a step ahead of the game, coming up with a solution.*

I also make a habit of visiting race shops from time to time, particularly on Monday mornings after weekends that have seen a lot of violent crashes. I'll examine the wrecked cars as closely as I can, trying to determine exactly what happened to cause the crash, what happened during the crash, and how the safety equipment performed throughout that whole process.

> **Rusty Wallace:** *I had a bad wreck at Bristol once where I flipped something like seven times. I had another bad wreck at Daytona in '93, where I flipped really violently on the backstretch. I had the worst wreck of my life at Talladega in '93. Just recently [July 1999] I had a bad crash at Pocono, where I hit the wall at 200 miles an hour damn near head-on, and walked away. Whenever something like this happens, it always seems like Simpson was one of the first guys to come by the shop the following week. He'll get in there and look through the car, asking me about things I hadn't even thought of.*

Sometimes I'll look at a crashed car and see something I think could be improved upon, even if the driver walked away in perfect health, and I'll relay that back to my people: "We need to change this." Happily, there are far more times when I'll see nothing wrong; everything worked exactly like it was supposed to work. In those moments I feel an indescribable satisfaction.

So my life is different now, but the general theme is the same. I still feel like this company is my child, even if its uncles and aunts at Carousel do most of the babysitting. And I still get a huge kick out of making sure we stay at the forefront of our industry.

*Rusty Wallace: There's one thing I know about Simpson: He cannot stand slackers. He hates anybody who does things half-assed or promises something they can't deliver. If one of his employees promises a customer something and doesn't come through, or if the quality of the merchandise isn't what Simpson thinks it ought to be, he goes nuts.*

*Bill Vukovich Jr.: I'll tell you how Simpson does things: When I worked for him he'd say, 'Have so-and-so send me a pair of size 10 shoes, but don't you dare let anybody know they're for me. Tell 'em the order is for some race driver.' That way, instead of having somebody cherry-pick the perfect pair for him, he'd get a pair straight off the assembly line. Then he'd look 'em over to make sure the quality-control people were doing their jobs.*

*Steve Krisiloff: His stuff was always absolutely the best it could be, and he was never satisfied until he got it to that point. Even today he'll pick up a helmet that's got some small flaw and he'll say, 'What happened here?' I mean, he can't look at every single piece that goes out, but if he happens to see something he doesn't like and it's got his name on it, he'll start raising hell. He is the ultimate quality-control guy.*

Right now, as we enter this new century, I feel like we're miles ahead of our competition. We've got things handled from the personal safety side and we're starting to look harder at expanding our horizons, including moving beyond personal safety and into areas like the general safety of racing facilities, which is an area that I think has too often been overlooked.

*Jim Williams: When we were building Irwindale Speedway I asked Bill if he would take a look at the place when he*

*got a chance. Well, he jumped right on his airplane and flew
to California. He and I walked the track together and as a
result of his input I repositioned some walls. With him this
safety stuff is a no-bullshit effort.*

For several years now I've been exploring what has come to be
known as the "soft wall" concept. The idea behind it is that the concrete retaining walls that line most of today's ovals have proven to
be too unforgiving, especially as speeds have climbed. In recent
years concrete has been looked upon as the great alternative to the
old steel guardrails. The guardrails did a terrific job of absorbing impact, but in violent crashes they sometimes came apart and pene-
trated the driver's compartment. Concrete tended to allow cars to
bounce away more cleanly, which solved that problem. Lately, how-
ever, we've seen another ugly problem arise: With chassis and tire
technology pushing speeds higher every season, cars are hitting the
concrete walls with incredible force, and the walls just don't have
any "give" to them. Rather than absorb the impact, they transfer it
back to the car and, ultimately, the driver. Too many guys have gotten hurt or killed lately after crashing into concrete walls, and that's
got to stop. Maybe we can't go back to guardrails, but there's got to
be something that absorbs impact like a guardrail and yet doesn't
come apart.

Right now there are half a dozen potentially viable impact-
absorbing systems being developed around the world, using everything from old tires to high-density foam to create a cushioning layer
between the race cars and the outside wall. I've been working hard
on one that relies mostly on tightly packed cardboard. One of these
things will, I believe, eventually catch on and lead to a new age in
track safety. Maybe in the future we'll look back at the notion of racing alongside bare concrete walls and shake our heads, the same
way today's drivers scoff at the idea of racing without fuel cells and
firesuits.

Everybody in the sport has worked awfully hard at making cars more crashproof, and I've spent most of my waking hours trying to make drivers more crashproof too. The next thing we ought to focus on, it seems to me, is making the walls more crashproof also.

Away from the tracks, we've developed a line of child car safety seats, based on what we've learned from years and years of perfecting restraining systems for race drivers. It's a neat little unit: The seat itself looks like a little racing bucket and it's got a set of belts built into it that resemble the ones Dale Earnhardt straps on every Sunday afternoon. Aside from the fact that it's really cool-looking, I'm proud of the fact that it's a step beyond the car seats families have been relying on for years.

And there's more. As this is being written we're developing a material that, for lack of a proper name, we call "green stuff." It's similar to the kitty-litter type of absorbing agent you see spread on race tracks after an engine blows, but it has one key advantage: It's the only material we know of that properly picks up *synthetic* oil. The existing products do a great job with conventional oil, but they don't completely absorb the synthetics. Well, our green stuff takes care of that.

And who knows? If this stuff makes race tracks safer, it can also make our highways safer, in regards to cleaning up anything from a minor accident to a huge wreck involving an oil truck.

Now, answer this for me: How the hell am I supposed to slow down, the way everyone expects me to, with all these neat things going on? I want to be around to see what happens next, whatever that might be.

When it comes to this business, I have never seen any end to the rainbow. I felt that way when I started Simpson Drag Chutes in 1958, I felt that way when I stepped out of a race car for the last time and went to work for real in 1977, and I feel that way at the dawn of the twenty-first century. In my opinion, Simpson Race Products can just grow and grow. I don't see a limit.

**Rusty Wallace:** *Bill Simpson is a damn good friend of mine, but that's not the reason I use his products. I use his products because he's such a racer-oriented guy. I was up at New Hampshire one time and I crashed. A few days later I said something to Bill about how hard I hit that wall. Well, he started looking at the way my helmet was fitting, making sure everything was right.*

*You know what it is with Simpson? He wants to make sure all his friends stay safe.*

# EPILOGUE

If you were around this sport 25 years ago and you claim today that you always knew it would get as big as it has, I'll call you a liar. I don't see how any of us — hot rod guys, drag guys, Indy car guys, stock car guys, any of us — could possibly have pictured what has come to pass.

Live racing on television every weekend? Forget it.

Serious coverage in every newspaper from the Los Angeles Times to the Wall Street Journal? Come on.

Sprawling new superspeedways near cities like Dallas, Chicago, Kansas City, Denver, Boston, Las Vegas? No way.

Sponsors on just about every car in the field? Yeah, right.

Multi-million-dollar point funds? Sure.

There was just no way to figure on any of this happening. If you were a racer back then, in almost any discipline of the sport, you could count on being an outcast, on traveling to tracks that always seemed run-down no matter how new they were, and on being broke. Racing was a hell of a lot of fun; we were pretty sure it would continue to be fun, we just never thought it would ever be a major-league deal.

Boy, were we ever wrong.

I'll show you how much racing as grown and how much growing it may yet do: We went through a period in the late 1980s when motorsports in general and NASCAR in particular were just starting to boom, when everybody went around saying, "The sport can't possibly get any bigger than this." In fact I said that myself as far back as the middle '70s; even then it seemed to me that things had just about topped out.

Well, nobody even ventures those kinds of predictions anymore. Even the pessimists concede that when it comes to racing's growth, we may have only seen the tip of the iceberg.

My son Jeff works for the Charlotte Hornets of the National Basketball Association and has contacts in other professional stick-and-ball teams, and Jeff has often told me that those guys are looking hard at automobile racing, trying to learn from the things that have made our sport so enormously popular. That's the ultimate compliment, a sure sign that we're doing something right.

And 10 years from now, if this upward spiral continues, what's going on then might make today's racing look small. Think about it: There are so many things going on that even we in the industry are not privy to.

Look at Speedway Motorsports, Inc. and International Speedway Corporation, which between them own most of the Winston Cup tracks and a large percentage of the Indy car tracks too. Who knows what big ideas are being tossed around in the boardrooms of those two outfits?

It doesn't stop there. Who knows what further improvements we might see in TV coverage? Who knows what sponsors may come on board to help this sport grow larger yet?

Racing has exploded to the point where it seems like everybody wants to get involved, including a lot of folks who wouldn't have given it a second glance 15 years ago. I mean, look how many young kids want to become race drivers these days, just because they've been exposed to it every week on TV.

In the old days most kids who started racing at a young age fit a certain pattern. They came from racing environments—maybe their dads or uncles or neighbors were drivers or mechanics—and they graduated from hanging around garages to driving quarter-midgets or hobby-level stock cars. It was a simple progression. They were born and brought up around the sport and it hooked them without them even realizing it.

Today a kid might grow up in a household that has no interest in motorsports whatsoever, but every Sunday he watches the Winston Cup or Indy car races and pretty soon he's hooked. At some point he talks his mom and pop into buying a go-kart and, boom, we've got another race driver on our hands. Maybe he's a future star, maybe he's just a mediocre talent; who knows? All that's for sure is that this kid would never have gotten involved with racing in the first place if it hadn't elbowed its way into the American sports mainstream.

Of course today there's another reason a lot of youngsters want to be race drivers: money. These kids want to be rich and famous, and if they're lucky they might get there. The best drivers can compare salaries and endorsement deals with professional baseball, basketball and football players; they are legitimate sports stars, and as such they have wealth and celebrity. There's no denying that all of this money is part of racing's allure these days.

But it's worth pointing out that it wasn't like this until very recently. I can assure you, guys like A.J. Foyt and Parnelli Jones and Snake Prudhomme didn't get into racing because they thought it would make them millionaires. They got into racing because something inside them drove them to.

> **Don Prudhomme:** *I'm sure most of us from back then, whether it was me or Simpson or Parnelli, weren't exactly Yale graduates. I'm sure most of us weren't particularly good in any form of schooling. I'm sure most of us weren't particularly good at football or baseball or any other sport. But, damn it, we were good at driving race cars. We found a niche in life and, wow, what a ride we had.*

It was the same with Dale Earnhardt. I met Earnhardt in 1978, a year before he won the Winston Cup rookie title, and the only thing I knew about him was that he had a reputation for being hard to get along with. We talked for a while and he didn't strike me as being difficult; what he struck me as, really, was a young guy who was more interested in being the best racer he could be than he was in all the other bullshit that went along with being a hero driver. I thought he was about as cool a sonofabitch as I had ever met, and I still feel that way. I mean, today Dale Earnhardt is a seven-time NASCAR champion and the whole world knows who he is, but he didn't get into this deal just to be a star and you could see that very clearly. He raced for all the right reasons and I respected that.

Happily, there are still plenty of kids out there who want to race for the same reasons we did, kids who would figure out a way to compete even if it didn't pay a dime. I look at them and in their eyes I see the same hunger I once had for driving race cars.

No, you don't see it in every driver. Just like when I came up, there are racers and there are hobbyists. There will always be guys who are out there just to have a little fun and there will always be guys who have blood in their eyes, who want very badly to succeed. By now I can tell which one of those camps a kid belongs in just by spending five minutes with him. One look at him and, most times, I know exactly what he's about.

Fifteen and 20 years ago I saw a fire in the eyes of guys like Michael Andretti, Pete Halsmer, Al Unser Jr. and Rick Mears. Ten years ago I saw that same fire in Davey Hamilton and in Parnelli's boys, P.J. Jones and Page Jones. In the last five years we've all seen it in Dale Earnhardt Jr., Tony Stewart and some of the other kids who are now starting to grab all the headlines.

And if you're a racer at heart and you're in a position to maybe help these guys—these kids with that wonderful fire in their eyes— you find yourself wanting to do whatever you can for them as they climb the ladder. In my case that has meant passing along a helmet or a fire suit or a few pairs of gloves, whatever it took to help move a kid's career along more easily.

*__P.J. Jones, Indy car and NASCAR driver:__ When my brother Page and I were just getting started, the big joke was that we needed our own drive-up window at the Simpson store in Torrance because we were there once a week for*

*visors, tear-offs, you name it. Bill was so good to us that my
mom made us take him presents on Father's Day. She called
him our surrogate father, and that's really how he treated us.*

Sure, this is kind of a two-way street. The businessman in me
hopes that if we help a young guy on the way up, he'll stay loyal to
our company if he becomes a big national name. But I'll be honest:
When I first take an interest in a kid, I do it more as a fan than as a
businessman. Like I said, I'm drawn to that fire in his eyes, that quality that makes him want to be better than the rest.

At that point that kid isn't out to be famous; he's out to win the
race. And, well, I just somehow find myself rooting for him.

> **Davey Hamilton, Indy Racing League driver:** *When I
> was racing supermodifieds it took all the money I had just to
> get from race to race, so safety became an area where I'd
> just get by with whatever I had. That was true even after I'd
> become pretty successful. Then, through Bill Vukovich, I met
> Simpson. We talked about the racing I had done and he asked
> about the kinds of things I wanted to do in the future. The
> next thing I knew, he started taking care of me. He helped me
> with safety equipment and he even helped me get rides. In
> fact the first Indy car ride I ever had, at Indianapolis in
> 1995, was something Simpson helped arrange with Chip
> Ganassi and Ron Hemelgarn. That deal was all Bill Simpson.
> I think he did it just because he's a racer at heart and he
> wanted to see me succeed.*

Lately I've been keeping an eye on A.J. Foyt's grandson, who
everybody calls Little A.J. The boy has been winning in go-karts and,
with the kind of coaching he's getting, he's bound to keep getting
better. I'm telling you, that kid is going to be a badass, just like his
granddaddy. He's still too young to drive on the street, but he's already got the kind of charisma most winners have. He talks like he

knows where he's going and nobody is going to get in his way, not even his grandfather.

With kids like little Foyt, it ain't about being rich or famous or comfortable. It's about being a racer.

And there are plenty of them around; all you've got to do is look and there they are.

For the last several years our company has been involved in sponsorship programs with USAC's open-wheel divisions, and whenever possible I'll go watch those guys at places like Indianapolis Raceway Park. Well, right from the time I walk into the pits I feel like I'm in heaven. I talk to all those young midget and sprint car guys, and I just love it. The best ones are more concerned with how fast their cars are than with how much the race pays, and that attitude is what makes them winners.

It sounds corny to say it, but it's true. These young hot dogs are the future of our sport. I take care of them when I can, but, again, it's more than a business deal to me. I look at a lot of them as friends, despite the difference in our ages, and I just like to be around them.

By the way, I'd like to think they look at me the same way. You know, sometimes when I show up at a short track I get treated like I'm some kind of a celebrity. Well, buddy, I ain't a celebrity and they don't need to treat me like one. I guess very few people in my position pay much attention to them, and maybe they're flattered by that so they go out of their way to be nice to me. But when it comes right down to it, I'm a racer just like they are.

I guess it was the racer in me that made me give car-owning another stab in May of 2000, when I joined up with Andy Hillenburg and some friends of his to field an entry in the Indy 500. I had met Andy back when he was driving sprint cars in Indiana, and we saw quite a bit of each other once he moved to Charlotte and started establishing himself as a stock car racer. When he decided to give the 500 a try, we bought a couple of used cars from John Menard and enlisted Tim Bumps and my old pal Wayne Leary to run the show.

Later, when it was pretty clear that our old cars weren't keeping up with the new-generation designs, I bought a 2000 model from Jeff Sinden and Joe Kennedy. We qualified for the race, which is never an easy thing at Indy, but it wasn't exactly a smooth month of May. We started 33rd and finished 28th after a wheel bearing let us down.

> **Andy Hillenburg, Indy Racing League driver:** *I had known Bill for 15 or 16 years and I think every time we talked about racing I mentioned that it was my dream to one day run the Indianapolis 500. So he knew how badly I wanted to do that. When it finally happened, I was happy that he was right there with me. He didn't exactly go out and get the ball rolling for me, and I didn't expect him to, but once I got things started with Preston Root and Usona Purcell, Bill jumped in and helped me finish off the deal. He got involved in a very big way and, really, that's what made it happen. If Bill Simpson hadn't come aboard I don't think our program would have gotten as far as it did. And, you know, I think the main reason he wanted to help me was that he identified with how I felt. As a driver he had once wanted to run Indianapolis that badly himself, and he did it.*

That Indy deal ended up costing me a bunch more money than I had ever figured on, but, hell, we had a bunch of fun too. We entered the car as The Sumar Special, in honor of the famous Indy cars of the same name that Preston Root's dad had campaigned in the 1950s, and we had a lot of neat people around: Leary was there, John Sears was bringing us lunches, most of the crew guys were friends of mine. We even got Jim Williams involved as a sponsor: On race day we had "Irwindale Speedway" painted on the sidepod. And we were all there for the right reason—for the sheer love of racing—which was what had brought me to Indianapolis as a competitor in the first place.

I guess my point is this: With everything our sport has on its side right now—all this growth, all these aggressive people in charge, all these bright young kids and all of us older guys who still have our whole hearts invested—its future looks terrific.

And me? Well, my future looks OK too. Nowadays, all my old pals say they're surprised that things turned out so well for me. I guess I've got to go along with that. In fact I'm not only surprised, I'm astounded. I was a wild-ass punk who never even got to high school, and here I am, having somehow reached 60, and things are pretty good.

> **Tom McEwen:** *I was always sure that Simpson had it in him to be successful. I just wasn't sure he was going to live long enough to amount to anything.*

> **Robin Miller:** *The great paradox about Simpson is that he loved being a clown and he was always partying and raising hell, but the guy had such a sharp mind and he was so safety-conscious. He was so far ahead of the curve. The guy was really brilliant. But back then I don't think anybody could have imagined that he'd amass the fortune he's made, that he'd be this incredible businessman.*

> **Roger Penske:** *Simpson was a guy who was always having fun. What nobody realized at the time was that he was a guy who would bring safety in all types of racing to a new level. He was a pretty shrewd character. I think maybe that other side of him was a facade, because he obviously knew what he was doing.*

> **Steve Krisiloff:** *Everybody always talks about, you know, "crazy Bill Simpson." But I'll tell you, he's crazy like a fox. He didn't get to where he is by being an idiot, OK? Maybe people see him in a bar, carrying on, but that's his way of releasing all his pent-up energies. During the day he's flat out, doing what he does best.*

> ***Jim Williams:*** *Somebody from the outside looking in, who only knows Simpson as the guy drinking the longneck bottle of beer, might be a little shocked at what he's accomplished. But if you really know him, you can't be shocked by what he's done. He might have stayed out late and he might have liked to have fun, but I don't think he was ever confused when it was time to do business.*

> ***Don Prudhomme:*** *To be honest, I never picked Simpson as a guy who was going to be somebody someday. Well, let me rephrase that; Because of the fact that he was just one of us, one of the hell-raising guys, I was surprised that he turned out to be as sharp at business as he is. I mean, he was making his safety equipment all along, so I knew he was smart, but I didn't realize he had what it took to be a businessman. But, God, has he made a lot out of himself.*

Financially speaking, I've seen hard days a few times in my life—once growing up and later because of the troubles I've already told you about—and I don't see myself ever going that far down again. Because, I'll tell you, I've been rich and I've been poor, and rich feels a whole lot better. I like my boat. I like my Learjet. I like my home on Lake Norman; I went so far over budget building it that I call it Rancho Costalot, but when I was done I had the house I wanted and there's something to be said for that.

> ***Wayne Leary:*** *Simpson has been at the top a couple of times and he's been to the bottom a couple of times. This is, I guess, the third time he's really had his shit together. He's always been able to build himself back up, and he's doing pretty well now.*

> ***David Lawson:*** *I knew Simpson when he had zero, and I have to say that even then he always appeared to have some*

> *money. What I mean is, whatever he had, he freely spent.*
> *Over time, as he became more successful, the spending got*
> *bigger. Now it's almost like funny money to him.*

I'm a firm believer in the idea that money isn't everything. It certainly doesn't rule my day-to-day life. Sure, I enjoy good food and I like fine restaurants, but it's unbelievable how often I find myself eating sandwiches in blue-collar bars in Charlotte or Indianapolis. That's where my friends are.

Some of those friends have been pretty successful too, and they've also made lots of money. But most of my pals are regular folks who hold down various jobs—usually in racing—and worry about their monthly bills. I don't give a damn about how rich or poor they happen to be; if I meet people who seem cool, I want to hang out with them. And that's the way I've always been.

I'm a pretty simple guy. I would rather wear jeans than an Armani suit and I don't particularly care what my friends wear.

Having said all that, I do believe there's a curtain that separates people in this country according to wealth. On one side of the curtain are working folks who struggle every day and never hold onto much of the money they've earned, and on the other side are the folks who eat caviar off silver spoons and wash it down with champagne. But I'm as comfortable on one side of that curtain as I am on the other, as long as I'm with people who enjoy having fun. I don't look at myself as being any better than a guy working in a fabrication shop for a stock car team, or a guy running a sprint car on some dirt track, just because my bank balance might happen to be bigger.

Sure, there are days when I say to myself, "Geez, I really do have a lot of money." But, hell, I never did anything just for the money, so I'm not going to let it start running my life now.

No, what runs my life is the mental and physical energy I put into keeping this company on top. That's not the calmest existence, by any means—I'm always moving, moving, moving, and sometimes it feels as if I live out of my airplane—but it has become a way of life.

My basic day involves getting up early and staying up late. I watch very little television and yet I rarely get to bed until one or two o'clock in the morning. At 11:00 P.M., when the rest of the world is shutting out the lights, I'm usually still designing new products in my head or trying to improve existing ones.

And don't think for a minute that I consider myself unique in having this sort of energy. Racing is unlike any other activity I'm aware of in that it mostly attracts so many folks who have a genuine passion for their work. I mean, if any of us who have made names for ourselves in this sport had devoted the same amount of time and effort to a business in the regular nine-to-five world, we'd have made the Gettys and the Rockefellers look like amateurs.

Billionaires, hell. They'd have to invent a new category to lump us under.

See, most of the people who succeed in racing, whether they've been formally educated or not, are as savvy and street-smart as any business leader you can name, but our edge is that we tend to work harder because we love what we do. I honestly believe this: You will not find a harder-working bunch of people anywhere than you'll find in the pit area at a major-league automobile race, from the best drivers to the top mechanics to the successful manufacturers. Racers love the process of problem-solving; instead of getting frustrated by new challenges, they get inspired, energized.

My own latest challenge has been trying to pass along to the people who now manage Simpson Race Products the things it took me 40 years to learn. I'm spending quite a bit of time with our new executives, getting them more familiar with the ins and outs of racing. Some of them knew this sport primarily from what they had seen on television; they'd never had any kind of real access to it. Now they accompany me to lots of races, which is good for two reasons: First, it allows them to see our products in practical applications; and second, these trips provide extra time for us to talk about things ranging from new items to marketing strategies. It's a way to help move the company forward.

And, you know, I've always looked ahead more than I've looked back. Maybe that was just the tinkerer in me; I knew that only by looking ahead and dreaming up new ideas could I ever hope to push the level of racing safety forward.

Not until I sat down to begin work on this book had I ever really pressed myself to dwell on my own past. But I'm glad I did because there are some pretty neat memories in there . . .

Like Mike Sarokin and me building parachutes on Haynes Lane in Redondo Beach. Every now and then when I'm out in California I'll drive past that old house and I'm always blown away. First of all, I'm kind of stunned that the thing is still standing. Second, I have a hard time believing how far I've come from that place.

Like hearing "Back Home Again in Indiana" on the Indy 500 grid in 1974. To this day, listening to that song still gives me chills.

Like raising hell with drag racers, Indy car racers, stock car racers, Grand Prix racers and sprint car racers from the late '50s right up until, oh, last night.

Like understanding how lucky I am and how easily things could have gone the other way. I think about the guys I knew over the years who are now dead. Some got killed in race cars. Some screwed themselves up with booze or drugs. Some just got old and that was that. And I'm still here.

Like seeing a hundred drivers climb out of crashes that might have maimed or even killed them, had it not been for some of the advances I helped push through.

There are plenty of good memories, for sure. I've had a lot of fun passing these along and I hope they helped you rekindle a few of your own. Like I said in the beginning, if you love racing this is your story as much as mine.

But now it's time for me to turn back toward the future. Because, see, I still feel exactly the way I did back in 1958: Racing isn't quite safe enough to suit me yet.

Maybe it never will be. But I'm not about to give up on that.

**Don Prudhomme:** *Sure, Simpson's done well financially. But when he was always telling us, "Hey, you guys need to wear these boots and these gloves because they're better," I never felt like he was just out to make a buck. I always believed he was trying to help us. And, goddam it, he did.*

# CONTRIBUTORS

*These men and women not only contributed the anecdotal memories that dot this book, but also provided invaluable background material. The authors extend their gratitude.*

- **BOBBY ALLISON** is one of stock car racing's living legends. The 1983 NASCAR Winston Cup champion, Allison, like Bill Simpson, has seen the sport grow from rough-and-tumble beginnings to its present glory days.

- **DENISE BELLE ISLE,** a secretary in Simpson's North Carolina office, often sees what Bill admits is his not-so-pleasant all-business side. And that's OK with her: "I like his boldness. Bill will say things other people wouldn't dream of saying."

- **DICK BERGGREN** is the executive editor of *Speedway Illustrated* magazine and one of America's most respected print and broadcast journalists. His staunch advocacy of driver safety, dating back more than 20 years, has kept him in frequent touch with Simpson.

- **LARRY BURTON** is a veteran mechanic who joined Simpson when the latter acquired his first Indy car, in 1968. He made several cross-country jaunts as part of Simpson's fledgling race team and served as Bill's chief mechanic in the Tasman series in Australia and New Zealand.

- **LINDA CONTI** used to be a trackside representative for Simpson Race Products, serving the Indy car and Formula One clientele. She is now an investment broker and financial advisor in Indianapolis.

- **A.J. FOYT** is often called the greatest American race driver. A four-time winner of the Indianapolis 500, Foyt also can claim victories at everything from fairgrounds dirt tracks to the Daytona 500 and the 24 Hours of Le Mans.

- **DAVEY HAMILTON,** a fixture in the Indy Racing League since 1996, is also one of America's most successful short-track racers. Included in his impressive resume are victories in supermodifieds, sprint cars and midgets.

- **C.J. HART** traces his involvement in drag racing all the way back to its roots. Now retired after a long stint as an official of the National Hot Rod Association, he helped stage some of Southern California's earliest organized drag races.

- **BILL HILDICK** met Simpson while helping spearhead the Norton Company's Indy car sponsorship. Later, through his work with the Portland, Oregon, Rose Festival, Hildick was largely responsible for launching that city's successful Championship Auto Racing Teams event.

- **ANDY HILLENBURG** drove a Simpson-backed entry in the 2000 Indianapolis 500, but the relationship between the two men spans Hillenburg's career in sprint cars and both ARCA and NASCAR stock cars.

- **PARNELLI JONES** is best known as the winner of the 1963 Indianapolis 500, but during his meteoric career he also won in NASCAR stock cars, SCCA Trans-Am road racers, US Auto Club midgets and sprint cars, and Baja off-road machines.

- **P.J. JONES** was born after his famous father had given up full-time competition, but the younger Jones inherited Parnelli's versatility. Now a NASCAR Busch Series racer, P.J. is also an Indy car veteran and a winner in IMSA sports cars, USAC midgets, and NASCAR trucks.

- **CHRIS KARAMESINES** owns one of the most important records in drag racing. This Top Fuel legend, also known as "the Golden Greek," is credited with being the first man in NHRA history to smash the 200 miles-per-hour barrier in a quarter-mile run.

- **STEVE KRISILOFF** drove in 11 Indianapolis 500s between 1971 and '83, placing fourth in 1978 and earning three other top-10 finishes. A former roommate of Simpson's, Krisiloff today works in the CART Champ car series for Patrick Racing, a team for which he once drove.

- **DAVID LAWSON** met Simpson some 30 years ago. Their friendship has endured a number of chaotic trips through Central and South America, including an unplanned stay in Havana after Simpson's boat strayed into Cuban waters.

- **WAYNE LEARY** can count the 1975 Indianapolis 500 and the '74 USAC Indy car national championship (both with driver Bobby Unser) among his accomplishments as one of the sport's craftiest wrenches. With 22 victories, Leary ranks sixth on the all-time win list for Indy car chief mechanics.

- **JOHN MARTIN** is a former Indy car driver and owner who, like Simpson, waged a valiant but futile struggle against runaway costs and technology in the early 1970s. Later he helped maintain a fleet of Simpson-owned Super Vee and formula cars.

- **TOM "MONGOOSE" McEWEN** rose from hot-rodding to become half of drag racing's first great rivalry. His epic quarter-mile wars against Don "Snake" Prudhomme helped put Funny Car racing on the national motorsports map in the 1970s.

- **RICK MEARS** won four Indianapolis 500s and three CART championships driving for Roger Penske, but his first Indy car ride was a Simpson-owned entry in the 1976 California 500. The two men became acquainted during Mears's off-road days and remain good friends.

- **ROBIN MILLER,** the always-opinionated lead motorsports columnist for the *Indianapolis Star*, was an eyewitness to many of Simpson's exploits (both on and off the track) during Bill's raucous Indy car driving days.

- **JOHN NICOTRA** spends his winters as a Florida produce broker and his summers following various racing series around the United States. His regular presence on the scenes has let him participate in many Simpson-inspired shenanigans.

- **ROGER PENSKE,** the most recognized car owner in American motor-sports, has fielded successful teams in USAC and CART Indy car competition, NASCAR stock car racing and SCCA road racing. Penske's cars have won the Indianapolis 500 an unmatched 10 times.

- **DON "SNAKE" PRUDHOMME** is another racing legend who emerged from Southern California's hot rod culture. Four NHRA Funny Car championships later, he is enshrined in the International Motorsports Hall of Fame and fields successful Funny Car and Top Fuel teams.

- **GARY ROVAZZINI** has seen the Indy car mechanic's life from both ends of the economic spectrum. He toiled for Simpson's underfunded team in the 1970s, but now is part of CART's well-financed Ganassi Racing juggernaut.

- **JOHNNY RUTHERFORD** is one of an elite handful of men who have won the Indianapolis 500 three times. Rutherford now works with the Indy Racing League, driving the pace car and mentoring aspiring Indy car racers.

- **JOHN SEARS** owns Kelly's Pub Too, a watering hole on the west side of Indianapolis, a part of the city known for its racing teams and personalities. Sears counts Simpson as both a longtime friend and a dedicated customer.

- **TOM SMITH** was a mechanic when Simpson's Indy car team was on the financial rocks. "With a little bit of ingenuity and a lot of hard work, we'd do all right," he says, "but we'd struggle." The two men remain friendly today.

- **TED SWIONKEK** was chief mechanic on Bill Simpson's only Indianapolis 500 start, in 1974. Though retired from active pit-crew duty, Ted still closes his auto-repair shop each May to make a pilgrimage to the Brickyard.

- **BILL VUKOVICH JR.** emerged from the long shadow of his father, 1954–55 Indianapolis 500 winner Bill Vukovich, to become one of the steadiest Indy car drivers of the '70s. Later, he worked as a race week-end representative for Simpson Race Products.

- **MARY WALKER** is the head secretary in Simpson's North Carolina office and also a sort of anger-management filter: "Bill recognizes that there are times when it's not a good idea for him to call someone. When that happens, it's my job to pass the message."

- **RUSTY WALLACE** has become one of the superstars of modern-day stock car racing. The 1989 NASCAR Winston Cup champion, Wallace is also a longtime Simpson friend. The two share ownership of a condo-minium at the Lowe's Motor Speedway in Charlotte.

- **JIM WILLIAMS** is the founder and owner of California's Irwindale Speedway. A Simpson pal for many years, his racing history includes a stint as an associate sponsor of Roger Penske's Indy car team. He is a former CEO of Golden State Foods.

MARK "BONES" BOURCIER has covered American automobile racing since 1976, contributing columns and feature stories to a number of national magazines and newspapers. His work appears regularly in *Speedway Illustrated* magazine, where he is a monthly columnist and editor-at-large. Bourcier is a two-time winner of the Miller Racing Award of Excellence in Honor of Russ Catlin, one of racing journalism's most coveted prizes, and a recipient of the Eastern Motorsports Press Association's Frank Blunk Memorial Award for outstanding journalistic contribution to the sport. He is also a multiple winner of the Feature, Column, and Personality Profile categories in the annual STP Writing Awards presented by EMPA. A Connecticut native, Bourcier now resides in Indianapolis.

LOMA MAR
QUARTET